"I believe an old fashioned word ı. ̣y.......

Angeles Arrien

"To me synchronicity is a combination of timing and events in the lives of people. It has something of the extraordinary to it, something we could not have created on our own, and something we become a part of in spite of ourselves."

Gloria Brown

"I see synchronicity as a dynamic intelligence beyond human comprehension that is interwoven into the web of life, so that life can maintain itself as a self regulating system. I believe it allows the connection between our mind and our personal day to day experiences, to be linked to the larger plan or the Universal Mind. It allows us to participate in life as a part of life. I think of it as 'cosmic arrangement'. It allows thoughts and beliefs to manifest the expressions they represent based upon the particular vibrational frequency of those thoughts and beliefs. I see synchronicity as a means that the universe utilizes to balance or fulfill what has been set into motion and as a means to support us on our journey of becoming soul conscious. I also feel that the concept of synchronicity is so profound that it is beyond our capability to fully grasp how the universe can possibly be that intelligent. I often find that with a synchronistic event, there are elements which have come together in a way that can defy statistical probability."

Ed Rubenstein

"My definition of synchronicity is when the unexpected happens just at the right time."

Arielle Ford

"Heaven is not a place far away, it is a dimension that coexists with the Here and Now . . . and we all have the ability to tune into this realm, through meditation or through slowing down the mind. Each person has inner dials that he or she can use to tune into a multitude of inner dimensions. Synchronicity starts to happen when you get close to the heavenly dimension. When you tune into that channel there is less lag time between a thought and the results or manifestation of that desire."

Denise Linn

"Synchronicities are little miracles through which an otherwise Unseen Consciousness communicates with us. We may speak to the gods in prayer, but significant coincidence is the medium whereby they speak to us."

Frank Joseph

"All things happen for a reason, synchronicities light up the path we are supposed to follow and it alerts us that we must pay attention to the opportunity the light is leading us to."

Raleigh Pinskey

"Synchronicity is a mystical coincidence of events that we later learn has great meaning in our lives."

Susan Miller

"Synchronicity is God's law of cause and effect. A tear in the fabric of 'the world of appearances' which allows the real world to shine through for just a moment. A synchronicity is a concrete sign in this world that comes from the one real world, the *unus mundus* back in behind this reality. It's the way your soul speaks to you, telling you that for that moment, you are on track with your life's plan."

Jacquelyn Small

"Synchronicity shows us there is a pattern and rhythm to things."

Dottie Walters

"Synchronicity is being at the right place at the right time for the 'Greater Good' and not realizing it until later."

Paola Harris

"Over the years we have learned to read signs and symbols from the Universe. We especially pay attention to messages from the crow and the owl. Our experiences have taught us that there are no accidents and true synchronicity is proof of this."

Amy Kees &
Dorothe Blackmere

"For me Synchronicity means the simultaneous occurrences of two events in one's life. Something that occurs at the same time or place which in most people's minds is a conincidence, but is it really? We begin to wonder about this and interpret . . . giving us reasons why events occur in our lives."

Suzanne Humes

"Synchronicity is best defined in our lives as signs and events that tweak our intuition, demanding that we pay attention."

Patrice Mattelon &
Kate Solisti-Mattelon

Synchronicity, Signs & Symbols

Patricia Rose Upczak

Synchronicity Publishing
Nederland, Colorado
www.csd.net/~synchron

Published in The United States of America
by Synchronicity Publishing
P.O. Box 927
Nederland, CO 80466

Cover Design by Gloria Brown

Interior artwork by Julia Lunk

Edited by Dr. Polly Palmer and Anne Elizabeth Upczak Garcia

Printed by Johnson Printing

ISBN# 1891554-19-0

Upczak, Patricia Rose.
    Synchronicity, signs & symbols / Patricia Rose
Upczak. -- 1st ed.
    p. cm.
    Includes bibliographical references.
    ISBN: 1-891554-19-0

    1. Coincidence—Psychic aspects. 2. Intuition.
I. Title.

BF1175.U63 2001   133.8
                        QBI01-200455

This book is dedicated to
my ancestors, my family and friends with deep gratitude.
Thank you for letting me travel with you through time.

Table of Contents

Acknowledgments

My life has been filled with synchronicity, signs and symbols. I treasure all the moments that have turned into years, with all the people who have helped me create this interesting tapestry I call my life.

I would especially like to thank all the people who have helped me with this book in any way shape or form. It is with deep gratitude that I acknowledge Angeles Arrien, Denise Linn, Frank Joseph, Arielle Ford, Jacquelyn Small, Raleigh Pinskey, Dottie Walters, Nancy Lee, Danielle Lin, Susan Miller, Jackie Olmsted, Polly Palmer, Alice Qualin, Marilyn Ross, Sandra Wales, Emily Rose Upczak, Deb Jordan, Gayle Seminara-Mandel, Kate Solisti-Mattelon, Patrice Mattelon, Dorothe Blackmere, Amy Kees, Anne Elizabeth Upczak Garcia, Gloria Brown, Sally Grahn, David Cole, Suzanne Humes, Russ Croop, Paola Harris, Joye Fuller and the Nederland Community Library.

Introduction

Synchronicity implies wholeness and meaningful relationships between causally unconnected events. Science has been rediscovering the view of the world as an unbroken fabric in which seemingly separate events do not occur in isolation, but form pieces interwoven into a common tapestry.

The idea of wholeness is emerging as a major theme of our culture. South African philosopher and statesman Jan Smuts articulated this view in his book *Holism* and *Evolution* back in 1926. He viewed the cosmos as formed of wholes, each interlacing with others to form larger, interconnected tapestries. He felt that these structures are not static but evolve toward increasingly inclusive, complex, and even creative forms. He called this picture of the universe of interwoven and evolving wholes "holism" after the Greek halo meaning whole.

This idea finds a modern version in biologist Rupert Sheldrake's theory of morphic fields, networks of resonance that form webs of mutual influence beyond the usual limitations of space and time.

On the level of popular culture, the notion of interconnection is seen in the story of the hundredth monkey, related by biologist Lyall Watson in his book *Lifetide: The Biology of Consciousness.*

Synchronicity bridges the gaps between the conscious and the unconscious, between the world of mind and the world of objective events. This book is filled with people's stories because synchronicity is ultimately best understood and comprehended through the stories of our lives.

Early in the 1900's synchronicity was investigated by Austrian biologist Paul Krammerer. He attempted to approach meaningful coincidences as objective physical phenomena. He was fascinated by events that repeated themselves too frequently to be passed off as chance. For example, on a particular day you

ix

notice that your lottery ticket bears the same three digit numbers as your train ticket which, in turn, is the same as the number on the taxicab that picks you up on the street corner and drops you off at your hotel, and the number of the address is the same three digit number, like 444.

This kind of unlikely sequence of·events fascinated and intrigued Paul Krammerer. He kept a log of such coincidences and wrote the book *Das Gesetz der Serie* in 1919. Krammerer believed that clusters of recurrent events grow in cyclic fashion like waves of water. Only the peaks of the waves are visible; everything else is too deep under the surface to be seen.

According to quantum physicist David Bohm, the entire Universe has to be understood as a single undivided whole. He also felt that the essential wholeness of the hologram is that each part contains or enfolds the whole, and that each part of the world contains the whole of the Universe hidden (enfolded) within it.

The Universe has two orders according to Bohm, the explicate order and the implicate order. Explicate order is the physical world as we know it on a day to day reality. The implicate order is the vast holomovement. Holomovement is a term that Bohm coined to describe the movement in the Universe. He felt that it described the dynamic actions of the Universe better than hologram because of the constant state of change and flux he felt was occurring. The notion of an implicate order is important to the understanding of synchronicity as it shows us that the cosmos has possibilities different from and greater than we had known or even suspected before. Thus, mystics and scientists are thrown together in the cosmic soup.

In every moment the universe is whispering to us. There are messages being carried on the winds. The morning songs of the birds outside the window, the sound of an ocean spraying the cliffs, or the babbling brook gurgling over rocks is waiting for us to pay attention. Ordinary, everyday happenings in our lives carry communication from the realm of spirit.

In the past, people understood and knew how to interpret these signs, symbols, and omens. Often the entire destiny of a tribe or nation was decided by signs. As technology and science became more disconnected from the concept of the world as a whole, people became more and more isolated from their connections to the earth and their inner wisdom.

The reason the story of the hundredth monkey is so popular is because it is now time to regain our lost ability to read and understand signs, symbols, and synchronicities in our lives. There is an accelerated awakening of planetary consciousness.

Many of the examples I use in this book were gathered from students in my workshops or interviews of some wonderful and gracious people. I have used pseudonyms in some of the examples and have for the most part used first names throughout. Several of the stories have been changed to respect the privacy of the people who told them to me.

Within each of us lives the ability to recognize and understand signs. This book can assist you in recovering your innate ability to hear the whispers of the Universe, and can help you make choices that will empower you and enrich your life.

"God is a sphere whose center is everywhere,
and whose circumference is nowhere."

- Hermes Trismegistus

Chapter 1

Listen to the Whispering of the Universe

The vastness of the Universe is beyond our comprehension. *Synchronicity, Signs & Symbols* is based on the premise that we live in a vibrant, alive, conscious, spiritual essence that whispers to us constantly at many levels. These whisperings can be dreams, animals, or birds crossing our paths, reoccurring numbers, and meaningful coincidences of all types that defy explanation. Synchronicity happens all the time, all over the world throughout time—what we call it matters not. History provides endless stories of our ancestors dealing with the unexplainable in their lives.

Most signs appear visually, but they can present themselves through sound, smell, touch, or appear as a hunch, an intuition, or even a dream. There are a number of ways in which your signs may appear to you. When you put a question or concern into the Universe, people who cross your path will often have a sign, message, or some significance for you. A good example of this is the following story. His name was Fleming, and he was

1

a poor Scottish farmer. One day, while trying to make a living for his family, he heard a cry for help coming from a nearby bog. He dropped his tools and ran to the bog. There, mired to his waist in black muck, was a terrified boy, screaming and struggling to free himself. Farmer Fleming saved the lad from what could have been a slow and horrible death. The next day, a fancy carriage drove up to the Scotsman's sparse surroundings. An elegantly dressed nobleman stepped out and introduced himself as the father of the boy Farmer Fleming had saved. "I want to repay you," said the nobleman. "You saved my son's life." "No, I can't accept payment for what I did," the Scottish farmer replied. At that moment, the farmer's own son came to the door of the family hovel. "Is that your son?" the nobleman asked. "Yes," replied the farmer proudly. "I'll make you a deal. Let me provide him with the level of education my son will enjoy. If the lad is anything like his father, he'll no doubt grow to be a man we both will be proud of." And that he did. Farmer Fleming's son attended the very best schools and, in time, he graduated from St. Mary's Hospital Medical School in London and went on to become known throughout the world as the revered Sir Alexander Fleming, the discoverer of penicillin. Years later, the same nobleman's son who was saved from the bog was stricken with pneumonia. What saved his life this time? Penicillin. The name of the nobleman? Lord Randolph Churchill. His son's name? Sir Winston Churchill.

Every person in your life is there for a reason. Start listening carefully to the people in your world; you may hear remarkable wisdom and life changing information.

The connections in our lives often are not made clear to us until years later through what appear to be random connections. A friend of mine, Jackie, told me this story—Her mother Frances, was born in Coudersport, a small town in northern Pennsylvania. As a young girl she was best friends with a girl named Helen. Helen's family shared a large home owned by a local family, the Olmsted's, who decided to sell the house and relocate. Helen had to move. As a token of her friendship Helen gave Frances a beautiful, cut glass crystal bowl that had been in the Olmsted family originally.

Frances met and married Robert Daily in 1935. They raised Jackie and her brother in Allentown, Pennsylvania. Years later Jackie went to school at the University of Colorado, met, fell in love with and married Conway H. Olmsted, Jr. Conway's grandfather was Marlin Edgar Olmsted from Coudersport, Pennsylvania. After Frances treasured her crystal bowl for over fifty years, it went to a new home in 1967, back to the Olmsted family—her daughter and new son-in-law.

A very powerful way in which signs filter into your consciousness is through random thoughts. Emotions can also be a clear source of information for us all if we pay attention to how we really feel about what is going on or what is being said.

There are so many ways we can become aware of signs or significant symbols in our lives. Signs come from songs, license plates, road signs, people, radio, television, movies, dreams and animals. In every culture human beings have received signs by observing the movements of the natural environment around them. From the way animals migrate, to the location of a lightning strike, to the shape of the clouds, nature constantly provides signs and symbols for us.

Accidents can create havoc in our lives, but in almost every case there is an underlying sign present at the exact time of the accident. I would like to point out, however, that the only person who can really ascertain what that sign or message means is the person involved. To develop your intuition and ask your higher self for clarity is very important .

If the Universe is a Divine Hologram, everything lives in God. We all experience God or Spirit at different vibrations and levels as we grow and develop. Accessing our multidimensional abilities and allowing the reality of the Universe to filter through our daily experiences is vital to our growth and progress as a soul. We all have our jobs or path each lifetime. We all have choices to make daily. We all have help in these choices, and it is up to us which path we choose and how fast our growth is on that path.

Carl Jung coined the term synchronicity to describe the coincidence of a concurrent physical and psychic event that defies the probability of chance and is meaningful to the observer. Jung felt that there was a realm beyond time, where matter, mind, and spirit merged as one. He felt that meaningful coincidences happened through some mechanism outside the realms of cause and effect.

As mentioned in the introduction, before Carl Jung, Austrian biologist Paul Krammerer documented another type of coincidence that he called "seriality" in which things repeat themselves across time. He was a fascinating personality who shone the spotlight on meaningful coincidences as a subject worthy of study. But, his approach didn't really show us the deeper meaning of the topic. Carl Jung provided the more intuitive approach that was required.

Jung sensed that meaningful coincidences were the surface effects of a deeper, more holistic reality. He used the medieval term *unus mundus* to refer to this unitary reality, the one world which exists behind the poles of matter and spirit.

He often referred to Schopenhauer as the godfather of his ideas on synchronicity. Schopenhauer wrote an essay *"On the Apparent Design in the Fate of the Individual,"* that dealt with the simultaneity of the causally unconnected which we call chance. It appears that many of Schopenhauer's ideas came from Leibnitz. Leibnitz was a great philosopher and mathematician in the late 1600's. According to Leibnitz the soul is a perpetual living mirror of the Universe.

His idea embraces the theory that the human soul contains a mirror reflection of the entire cosmos in miniature, which refers to the theory that our Universe is a Divine Hologram, and that we are all totally connected. Some of our greatest minds are coming to the same conclusion, each contributing their part to the whole. Candace Pert, author of *Molecules of Emotion,* pioneered studies in molecular biology that have opened up a whole new world at the microcosmic level. Scientists David Bohm and Rupert Sheldrake have contributed to the understanding of synchronicity through their studies and work in quantum physics. Their work is helping this planet and our understanding immensely.

According to Frank Joseph, author of *Synchronicity and You,* "synchronicities are little miracles through which an otherwise Unseen Consciousness communicates with us. We may speak to the gods in prayer, but significant coincidence is the medium whereby they speak to us."

Jacquelyn Small, renowned author and lecturer, defined synchronicity as "God's law of cause and effect. A tear in the fabric of the world of appearances which allows the real world to shine through for just a moment. A synchronicity is a concrete sign in this world that comes from the one real world, the *unus mundus* back in behind this reality. It's the way your soul speaks to you, telling you that for that moment, you are on track with your life's plan."

Learning about synchronicity can be likened to putting on 3-D glasses that allow totally new dimensions to pop out when you look over your life. Once you know what synchronicity is and how to look for it, you begin to notice it everywhere. It reminds us that we are not alone, and that we have help along our path from a divine source.

Synchronicity shows up in your life and has patterns in single incidence, strings, and clusters. People most often experience synchronicity when they are open and aware, which in turn is affected by the outer conditions in which they might put themselves.

Special circumstances such as death, birth, and times of crisis or upheaval are outer conditions that push us towards openness, because when life becomes unpredictable we feel more vulnerable. Turning points, personal crises, falling in or out of love, rescues from danger, travel, and past life experiences are times when worries of daily life recede as we are drawn into the currents of a larger existence.

Our senses and awareness are heightened during times of turmoil, change, and challenge. When we are searching for solutions or learning how to adapt to unexpected joy and happiness, we are much more open to input from all sources. Synchronicity reassures us, points us in a whole new direction, or gives us the missing piece we need to make everything work. Turning points occur, and we question our future. What lies ahead? What can we do about it? Often in these times, synchronicity appears in dramatic ways. It moves us along, and it gives us a sense of reassurance and certainty about what we're doing.

The more deeply we understand synchronicity, the more we'll be able to see the different ways that the Universe talks to us. Full comprehension of the language of synchronicity prepares us to recognize it in all its manifestation.

In this day and age when our planet is in crisis, and things appear quite bleak, I want to address the importance of each individual's energy. There are no accidents, all make a difference, and our choices are important. What each individual does will contribute to the whole, and eventually change will be seen in a dramatic way.

Synchronistic experiences point to a profound relationship or interconnection between all parts of the Universe. These experiences surprise and confound the purely rational mind, because most people do not have a framework for random happenings that seem to fit our needs beyond coincidences. We must learn that the Universe does provide us with the tools to follow our destiny.

In the fall of 1997 I attended the Body and Soul Conference in San Francisco where I heard many wonderful speakers give presentations. One story stood out, and I knew I needed to pay attention to it. James Redfield was talking about how important it is to follow synchronistic nudges from the Universe. He referred to a story about Abraham Lincoln. As the story goes, an old peddler, who was down on his luck, came to Abraham Lincoln one day with a barrel of goods. The peddler told Lincoln he would sell him the whole barrel for a dollar. He told Lincoln he really needed the dollar. Lincoln "knew" that the contents of this barrel weren't worth a dollar, for it appeared to have only old canned goods in it. But he had compassion for the old peddler and gave him the dollar for the barrel. Some time later when Lincoln finally got around to clearing out the barrel, he found a complete set of law books at the bottom. According to Ira Progoff in his book *Jung, Synchronicity, and Human Destiny,* these law books were *Blackstone's Commentaries.* It was the synchronistic acquisition of these books that enabled Abraham Lincoln to follow his destiny, become a lawyer, and eventually president.

Joseph Campbell describes the miracle of what he called the "helping hands" phenomenon in his book *The Power of Myth.* The basic concept of this phenomenon is that when we ask God for help, all of a sudden people and opportunities show up out of the blue to help us accomplish what we are trying to do.

Publicist and author Arielle Ford believes strongly in synchronicity. She defined synchronicity as occurrences that happen unexpectedly at the right time. A significant event happened to her one day over nine years ago when a friend asked her who her dream client would be. She answered instantly "Deepak Chopra." He said, "Well, I have a friend who works with him and I'll give you her phone number—maybe you can get a meeting with him." She was quite surprised because she didn't think he had even heard of Deepak. So she called Patrick's friend, Penny, and explained who she was and why she was calling. Penny told Arielle that it just so happened that Dr. Chopra was thinking about hiring a publicist AND he would be in Los Angeles the next week. Penny arranged the meeting, and in a brief ten minutes Arielle told Dr. Chopra that he was one of the best kept secrets in the country, and that if he wanted to help more people then he should hire her. He said okay. They have now been working together for over nine years.

This is a perfect example of Joseph Campbell's helping hands phenomenon, as is Elizabeth's story of a summer to remember. Many years ago Elizabeth and her family were dealing with a great deal of turmoil in their lives. They had to put all of their belongings in storage for a summer and were living with family members in San Diego while Elizabeth finished her Masters Degree. That summer was a lesson in strange events, angels, and synchronicities.

Elizabeth's uncle became very ill right after her family came back to San Diego. Within a week he was in a coma. Elizabeth started driving her aunt back and forth to the hospital everyday, which was hard because she also had to take care of her family (which was almost fifty miles away from her aunt and uncle's home) and go to school.

One night Elizabeth was driving home at 2:30 a.m. after a grueling day. She was driving down a deserted highway and fell asleep. All of a sudden Elizabeth woke up with a start because of a high pitched sound and brilliant green light that filled her car. The light was like being in a fog. She slammed on the brakes and rolled down the window. She had to wipe off the window from the inside of the car. Fifty feet ahead of her stopped car was a huge concrete construction barrier that she would have hit within seconds.

To this day Elizabeth believes that green light was an angel protecting her. Her uncle died that week, and her family went back to Colorado. When they got there, they couldn't find any place to rent. Every place they went, they were either too late, couldn't afford it or they were rejected because they had children and a small Border Collie. They were living in a small motel and running out of money. So when a friend of theirs told them about a note he had seen for a little house up in the mountains, and that they only rented to teachers (she and her husband were teachers) it sounded too good to be true. Elizabeth was so discouraged she almost didn't go look at the house. But Elizabeth and her family did go, and they met Sally, a woman who to this day is a very close family friend. Much to their surprise this house was on two acres, cost eighty dollars a month, and they had no rules about children or dogs. Elizabeth learned that sometimes we get many "no's" while the Universe is getting something much better for us, and we need to be willing to stay open and pay attention when the right thing does come along.

In researching this book I discovered that Elizabeth's story was not unique. We all have fascinating experiences that defy rational thought. Our connection to the Divine is much greater than most people would like to admit. It gives all of us the power to heal our lives at deep levels if we are open to the signs and symbols being given to us daily.

As dawn approaches and the veil between night and day is lifting, I observe the crescent moon as it hangs elegantly in the sky, reminding me of other worlds, other dimensions that are the reality of the Universe. The miracles of life all happen without any effort from me, and yet somehow they interact with my existence. The labyrinth at Grace Cathedral in San Francisco calls out to me from another dimension that calms and heals me. The spirals and shapes of the Universe weave an intricate story filled with wisdom and mysteries. They beckon to us— whispering gently to investigate the reality that is just beyond our reach.

We are given knowledge in pieces, in steps so that we can grow in understanding. Our ability to open our minds and flow with the Universe is vital for our development.

Ostenta are signs in the natural environment that usually comment on what is happening right now or foreshadow those to come. The Etruscans coined this word. They interpreted the direction of the wind at a particular moment, cloud designs, and patterns in lightning, much as did the native people of many cultures.

Ostenta involve the entire range of natural phenomena from animal behavior to geologic and meteorologic occurrences. According to Frank Joseph, "If interpreted properly those acausal incidents in nature reveal what appear to us, from our narrow perspective, to be future events. For synchronicity implies that our linear concept of time is only relative to our earthly existence. The Universe runs on a different timetable and breaks through to or interfaces with our human realm only in instances of meaningful coincidences."

Angeles Arrien is an expert on the symbolic world. She researched the origins of over twelve hundred different symbols, finding that five basic shapes appear in the art of all cultures, and that people of different cultures give similar meanings to these shapes. Angeles defined synchronicity as a new term for what she calls grace. She believes that it happens to everyone, and the trick is to still our mind and pay attention to all the messages we get from Spirit. When she was in her late twenties sitting on some steps lost in thought about the possibility of going to graduate school, she had an experience that she felt changed her direction in life dramatically. She was thinking that she could only go to school if she could take something that included music, art, philosophy, and cross cultural studies when a young man walked up to her. He asked her, "What are you thinking about?" and she said, "Nothing." He said, "No, I'm serious, what are you thinking about right now?" So she told him and he said, "I know what that is." He pulled a college catalog out of his backpack, pointed to Cultural Anthropology, and gave her the catalog. When she looked up in amazement, he had disappeared. She enrolled at U.C. Berkeley the next fall. To this day she believes that this was a divine messenger sent to guide her when she was at a major crossroad in her life.

Denise Linn is a internationally known author and healer. She feels that signs are a focal point through which the cosmos filters into our physical reality. She suggests that it is very important for people to learn to interpret signs, symbols, and coincidences for themselves. Some of the ways she suggests are as follows:

1) Develop your own intuition.
2) Take note of the feeling that you associate with the sign.
3) Make a sign or synchronicity journal.
4) Ask your guides and angels for help.
5) Use a sign dictionary to become familiar with common meanings.

Denise had a Taos Pueblo Indian teacher named Dancing Feather, who was very important in her life. She was with him as he lay dying in the Santa Fe Indian Hospital. His last words to her were, "Wherever you are, wherever you go, I will be there." After his death, feathers began to appear to Denise in the most unusual places. She soon accepted that these feathers were signs or messages from Dancing Feather and the realm of Spirit. Feathers came when she needed assurance that she was on the right path.

Sometimes the feather signs came in ordinary ways, such as during a walk through a park; sometimes they would appear in mysterious, unexplainable ways. One night she was having a very difficult time, and she had to get ready to do a presentation the next morning. So she got up before dawn and filled the bathtub with water. Her head hurt, so she only lit a candle in the bathroom. While she was in the tub she became aware of something large floating in the water with her. She got out and turned on the light. It was a large, beautiful, white feather. The windows were closed, and she knew that feather was not there the night before. She relaxed and knew it was a sign from Dancing Feather that she would do fine at the presentation.

Internationally known speaker Dottie Walters told me a wonderful story about her first major speech in front of 5000 people. She walked out, and looked at the audience, and froze.

She said she was so scared that she didn't even have the strength to run off the stage. So she remembered a pink blanket that she used to give her children when they were young and had a really hard day or trauma. They used to curl up in that pink blanket and it made them feel better. So she visualized all those people in her pink blanket, and suddenly words poured out of her, consequently she did a wonderful job speaking. Afterwards a woman came up to her and told her that in the beginning she didn't like Dottie at all, but from the time that the big pink spotlight came on her, she really enjoyed the speech and Dottie. Dottie said she was stunned because there wasn't any spotlight on her at all.

Many of the people I interviewed have had remarkable and strange experiences while speaking in front of a large audience. Denise Linn told me that once while she was talking about her synchronicities with feathers, one large feather floated down from the ceiling right in the middle of her speech. James Redfield gave the people in his audience at the Body and Soul Conference advice for seekers of truth. He told us that it is very important to follow the path that the synchronicities are leading you to. His advice about learning to see auras also intrigued me. He said, "if you want to see auras, go hang out with people who do, and pretty soon so will you." This comment fascinated me for a number of reasons. There have been a number of studies around learning and how it is transmitted from one member of a species to another without any direct communication or even contact.

A number of scientists have studied animals and their ability to learn or know tasks without contact with the trained animals. One famous example of this remote "shared learning" occurred in Britain, where milkmen for over one hundred years have left bottles of milk undisturbed at the doors of homes in the early hours of dawn. But in 1921 this all changed. Rupert Sheldrake discusses the behavior of a small bird called the blue tit in the town of Southampton, England in his book *The Presence of the Past*. A small number of these birds learned how to open bottles of milk. There were even reports of blue tits following delivery trucks and breaking into bottles while the drivers made deliveries. By 1937, eleven species of birds had begun this activity, and it spread to eighty nine different cities in England. Then the jump occurred. A certain critical mass appears to have been achieved in Britain, because suddenly blue tits in Sweden, Denmark, and Holland began to attack milk bottles in the same fashion. It was impossible that this could have been learned behavior or something that these birds observed.

Strangely enough, milk bottles were not used in Holland during the years of World War II, and were only reintroduced in 1947. None of the blue tits alive then could have ever seen a milk bottle, and yet as soon as the milk bottle reappeared the blue tits began to attack them. Certain facts point to Sheldrake's theory of morphic resonance in the spread of this behavior. First, blue tits are birds that do not usually travel far from their breeding place; but the habit of opening the milk bottles appeared at a number of locations far from the previous cities. Sheldrake estimated that the habit must have been rediscovered independently at least eighty-nine times in the British Isles alone. Also, as the habit began to be practiced by more numbers of birds, it spread with increasing speed, suggesting a quantum leap as numbers increased.

Another famous story that was written about by biologist Lyall Watson in his book Lifetide: *The Biology of Consciousness* and then popularized in Ken Keyes' book The Hundredth Monkey occurred off the coast of Japan in 1952, on the island of Koshima. Scientists studying the behavior of a local band of monkeys, Mucaca fuscats, began to feed them by dropping sweet potatoes in the sand on the beach. The sand made the potatoes difficult to eat, and one young female, Imo, learned to wash the potatoes before eating them. She taught this behavior to her friends and relatives, and pretty soon many of the monkeys were imitating Imo's food washing behavior. The scientists observed this with interest, watching how the behavior slowly spread through the tribe, until one day something star-tling happened—every monkey in the tribe began washing their food. The scientists reported their observation—at the same time that another group of scientists at Takasaklyama on the distant mainland had noticed an odd and eerie phenomenon: suddenly all the Macaca fuscata monkeys they were observing had begun to wash their food in the ocean with no physical con-nection to Imo or the original band of monkeys.

We have been told throughout time that "Energy follows thought." What we think about all day long, what we focus on creates our reality and our life on this planet. As you look around, you will see many people working for change in a pos-itive way. For instance, *A Course In Miracles* is being translated into numerous languages throughout the world, because people are ready for change. We have seen alternative medicine gradu-ally make its way into the mainstream of health care options in the western world. Major book stores now feature large sections on new consciousness. Even businesses and corporations are talking about "Spirit." It should come as no surprise then that *A Course In Miracles* was recently introduced at a historic gath-ering of the world's religious and spiritual leaders which took place at the United Nations. Delegates pledged to work for peace by signing a document titled *"Commitment To Global Peace."* These delegates included a group of indigenous people from the Amazon jungle in Brazil. When asked to sum up the meeting, Mr. Bawa Jain, the Summit's Secretary General said, "It's a Course in Miracles." Teachings from *A Course In Miracles* were included in the summit events and a prayer of forgiveness was used from the Course at the closing ceremony.

There seems to be a great push to get the *Course* and its rep-resentatives in the UN. All spiritual traditions were represented at the Peace Summit. *A Course In Miracles* has been introduced to prison programs in both Mexico and the USA, and since the summit, the Course's international center has been flooded with requests from around the globe.

"Remember that everything has God's
fingerprints on it."

- Richard Carlson, Ph.D.

Chapter 2

Synchronicity and Nature

Synchronicities, signs, and symbols are at their most potent in the realm of plants, animals, and insects. In his autobiography, Nikos Kazantzakis, author of *Zorba the Greek,* described an incident in which he came upon a cocoon cradled in the bark of an olive tree just as the butterfly was making a hole and attempting to emerge. Impatient for results, he bent over it and warmed it under his breath, by which he succeeded in speeding up the process. The butterfly, however, emerged prematurely, its wings hopelessly crumpled and stuck to its own body, which needed the sun's patient warmth, not the man's breath, to transform it. Moments later, after a desperate struggle, the butterfly died in the palm of his hand. "That little body," he wrote towards the end of his life, "is the greatest weight I have on my conscience."

Patience and openness is the missing link in the discernment process. As we search for guidance and clarity in our lives, the Universe will guide us. It is our job to be still, observe, meditate, and take long walks in nature where the answers to our questions will gently unfold.

It was early spring as Susan did her meditation in the late afternoon. She heard a thump and flutter against her sliding doors.

Finally, because the sound persisted, she got up to investigate and, much to her surprise a huge, beautiful mourning dove was trying to get into her home.

She had lived in her mountain home for almost twenty years and had never seen a dove at her bird feeder. It filled her with unexplainable joy and happiness. The following week as Susan was getting ready for work she glanced out her sliding glass door at the beautiful hues of a rose, and orange sunrise. Much to her surprise there were six beautiful doves eating at her bird feeder. Again, a feeling of peace and calm came over her for no reason except the birds made her happy.

Later that summer, the doves started showing up regularly in larger numbers. She was sad when fall came and they all left for the winter. Almost like a present the following spring, as she dealt with the ups and downs of her life, the doves returned; only this time she counted anywhere from twelve to twenty of them at a time. They circled her home and sat in the trees near her deck or at her bird feeders.

Each time she saw them that feeling of peace and calm came over her. So one day she decided to look up "dove" to see what it might mean, and this is what she discovered. Dove is a sign of peace and love. Dove wisdom brings understanding of gentleness. The dove is considered a spirit messenger. The legends and lore surrounding the dove connect it with many goddesses. It is a bird of prophecy and can help us see what we need to let go of, and what we need to give birth to in our life.

She felt as if this definition were a powerful description of what was going on in her life at that time. She considered the appearance of the doves a great gift from the Universe.

Over the years I have always sent small donations to the Salesian Missions because they help so many people throughout the world. There is a remarkable story from the life of St. John Bosco (1815–88), the founder of the Salesians, that has always intrigued me. Don Bosco was from Turin, Italy and he spent his life rescuing homeless boys in Italy. He founded places in Italy for them to live, learn a trade, and go to school. Strangely enough because he took the boys off the streets and taught them ways to earn a living, some of the businesses could no longer exploit them as day laborers. Their profits were reduced and they were angry.

Don Bosco walked alone at night through dark alleys to find the homeless boys, unafraid. One night as he started to walk home, two men pounced on him. It became clear they were hired assassins to get rid of this troublesome priest. As Don Bosco struggled to free himself from the cloak they had thrown over his head, he heard a deep, menacing growl. Before the men could move the priest, a huge gray dog leaped at them. Both men fell to the ground yelling, "Don Bosco call off your dog!" He answered, "Take this cloak off my head." At that the dog backed off and waited quietly. The men released Don Bosco and ran away.

The large dog waited and walked with Don Bosco until he got home. When Don Bosco got home, he opened his door and motioned for the dog to come in with him, but as soon as he was safely inside, the big gray dog was gone. Don Bosco asked throughout the area if anyone had seen this huge gray dog who had saved his life. He called him Grigio, which is Italian for gray. No one had ever seen him, which seemed impossible for such a large animal.

As the Don Bosco story continues, every time after that first dangerous incident, the gray dog was waiting to go with him, staying close until Don Bosco was safely home. Then he would disappear. This continued until Don Bosco and his work could be conducted safely without protection. It is said that Grigio showed up one last time, as if to say goodbye, because his work was done with this saintly man.

Kate, author and animal communicator, told me the following wonderful story. She said that any time a wild animal crosses her path, she asks for a message. Either they tell her or she finds the information she is looking for in the *Medicine Cards,* or Ted Andrews' book *Animal Speak.* She told me that every animal is a messenger, if we take the time to ask and listen. The other day she was driving home from dropping off her daughter at school and two quail ran under her car. The male made it, but the female didn't. She was in tears. She picked her up and "reiked" her. The male was distraught. She asked for forgiveness and sent them all the love she could. The next morning first one quail, and then his mate jumped over her fence and stayed in their backyard for about twenty minutes. It was a beautiful gift of forgiveness for her. The lesson was about not blaming herself for the choices of others, and that life and love go on.

Another important animal symbol that is prevalent in peoples' lives is the turtle. Turtles have lived on our planet for over 200 million years. Symbolically the sea turtle stands for success, achievement, creative progress, and attainment of our goals if we persevere. When the sea turtle appears, either in pictures or real life, we are being told that the worst is over, and as long as we maintain our persistence and courage success is assured. The sea turtle also alerts us to find a balance between practicality, creativity, care, and patience.

Tortoises are land turtles. They usually indicate that problems can be solved through patiently dealing with things one step at a time. They tell us to slow down and focus on the basic parts of our lives. They often appear when we have been experiencing many changes, burdens, and hardships. They remind us that there is light at the end of the tunnel and that success is within our reach if we persevere. In Native American cultures the turtle is the oldest symbol for our planet, Mother Earth. Throughout my life I have been drawn to turtles of all types. I especially love the sea turtles and the large tortoises.

Linda told me some wonderful stories about her experiences with birds and animals, a significant one which is with the eagle. Some years ago her life was in major turmoil. She had gone through a difficult divorce and had some important decisions to make about her life and her home. She walked out to a large rock outcropping that overlooked a valley near her home. As she sat there crying she begged the Universe for guidance and help. Suddenly two large golden eagles started circling about thirty feet above her as she sat on this rock overlook. She knew in that moment that somehow she was on her right path. Later in that same week, much to her delight, a pair of eagles circled her home for about a half an hour. She was touched and encouraged by their power, elegance, and grace.

In ancient Egypt the eagle was the symbol of the day, the light of the sun, and the sign of illumination. According to indigenous cultures around the world the eagle is a symbol of the Creator. The eagle connects us to the Great Spirit above. In many ancient cultures the eagle was seen as a messenger from the heavens.

An eagle can signal a time of power, strength, and soaring freedom in our life. It might also be telling us to look at some situation from a higher perspective, to go up above our troubles and see the bigger picture.

High in the rugged alpine forests of the Rocky Mountains, Barbara considered herself blessed to see many different types of wildlife. It was common for her to hear the owl call out through the stillness of the night. Barbara considered the owl her friend. One cold, wintry night as she drove up her long dark driveway, a huge owl flew directly over her car and ahead of her into the car lights. It was a sight that made her tingle all over. Years later one April evening at dusk, Barbara was in her kitchen talking on the phone to a person she considered her soul mate. Things hadn't been going well, and as she talked to him she wondered what would happen to them. Just as she had that thought, a giant horned owl landed on her deck railing and just sat there staring at her for over ten minutes. She knew that somehow she was being told that things would be okay and to use the wisdom of the owl around her concerns.

Symbolically, owls are one of the major birds recognized around the world and can represent the following: transformation, rebirth, ancient wisdom, death, seeing clearly where things seem dark and profound insight. Athena, the Greek goddess of wisdom, was depicted as having an owl on her shoulder that revealed inner truth to her.

Several years ago Denise Linn was at the International New Age Trade Show in Denver, Colorado, signing books and giving talks. At her booth she had given away some sample CD's of her meditations. So that night I relaxed and listened to the CD. Somewhere in the middle of these meditations I had this amazing vision of the space filled with stars. Suddenly a giant, sparkling white feather appeared, and then slowly Denise's face came through behind the white feather. Well this didn't make sense to me and honestly didn't mean anything to me at the time. So the next day my daughter and I were at Denise's author lunch, and she asked if anyone had any questions. So I asked her about this strange vision I had during her mediation CD. She looked at me rather startled and said, "Do you know what my spiritual name is?" I said "No". After a pause she said, "It is White Feather." So when I interviewed her she told me about her connection to the Great Horned Owl and how she got her spiritual name. She had a profound experience in the woods of the Cascade Mountains of Washington State. Golden late afternoon light streamed through the rich canopy of leaves overhead, as Denise closed her eyes and plaintively asked the Creator for her spirit name. When she opened her eyes, she was astonished to see a great horned owl sitting just three feet away from her on a branch at eye level. She said that she felt something deep and primal within her shift, as she and the owl maintained eye contact. Then just as silently as it appeared, it slipped away soaring into the forest shadows. On the branch where it had been sitting, it left three white feathers, and Denise knew her spirit name was White Feather. From that point in Denise's life, owls (and feathers) have been a very significant sign for her.

One time Denise was sitting in her home in Seattle thinking about the symbology of owls, and suddenly a great horned owl about 2 1/2 feet tall landed in the tree right outside her window. Denise said, "It was especially amazing as this occurred on a sunny day at 3:00 p.m. in the afternoon. The owl was only a few feet away from where I sat . . . it just stared at me." She was so excited that she sent her daughter outside to look at it. She didn't want to move, for it was so close to her as she was watching it. As her daughter did this, a large black crow landed in the same tree about a foot and half from the owl and also sat there staring at Denise. They stayed there for about a half hour. (Denise told me that once you start working with a certain animal as part of your totem they will help you forever, and she had started working with the crow since she had done work with Australian aborigines.)

Denise has recently moved to California and she is quite pleased because there are two great horned owls that live in the 100 year old oak tree in her yard and they hoot every morning and evening. Denise mentioned that she continues to work with both owl and crow "medicine." She told me that they show up whenever she needs help, encouragement or wisdom in any way.

The crow is a very powerful sign. The crow is thought to have mystical powers and to be a messenger from the spiritual realm. Change is always on the way when a crow shows up in your life. You also might consider changing the way you view reality and the inner realms or worlds. In some traditions crows are feared because they have associations with death. However, in Persian culture the crow brings good luck.

Gayle, owner of Transitions Bookplace in Chicago, told me a wonderful story about her struggles to keep the store open. They had Andrew Weil come to speak, and things didn't go as well as she wanted. It was a particularly hard time; she had become very discouraged and wondered if she and her husband should keep the store open. They had mortgaged their home, and it was such a financial struggle, she wasn't sure it was what they were supposed to be doing with their lives. She was sitting in a little coffee shop eating her lunch, asking for a sign of some kind so she would know what to do; just at that moment she looked out the window into an empty lot filled with cans and debris. Right in the middle of all of Chicago's traffic and turmoil was this beautiful, tall, strong sunflower with a beam of sunlight shining on it. She knew that this sunflower was her answer. No matter how hard it was to keep the store open, she knew in her heart that this bookstore filled a very important need, and that things would turn out just fine if she just kept going. Transitions Books is now one of the country's most well known metaphysical bookstores, because she paid attention to a sign that came to her. In many cultures the sunflower is a symbol of God's love. It is also a sign of joy, and its message is to embrace the fullness of joy. In many cultures the sunflower is thought to have magical powers. In China the sunflower represented longevity and magic.

Many of the people I interviewed felt connected to butterflies, wolves, and snakes. The butterfly is a wonderful symbol of transformation and change. Butterflies are supposed to stand for freedom, clarity of mind, energy to finish projects, and help in taking the next step in your life with the proper timing.

Wolves are also a very powerful symbol. Wolves are connected to protection, family, teachers, psychic powers, and loyalty. I spoke to one couple that had a wonderful story about the positive energy around the wolf as a symbol. James had always felt connected to wolves, so much so that he had a wolf tattooed on his ankle. Then one day, long after he had this tattoo done, he met the love of his life, Rose. They fell in love and are still together now, years later. Just recently they discovered that Rose's last name in its original form back in Poland meant keeper of the wolf.

Snakes have been significant symbols throughout history. Snakes stand for transmutation, healing, kundalini energy, resurrection, and transformation. Kate and Patrice have numerous experiences with both of these animals, either in real life or in their dreams, and feel very connected to them in a positive way. Many people are afraid of both wolves and snakes, but generally they are not fearful as signs or symbols. Nancy Lee, a well known talk radio show host, told me about her unique experience in Sedona, Arizona, with a snake. She and some friends were on a journey, and they couldn't find the people they were supposed to meet. As they were driving out of town a large snake went across the road in front of their car. Being very intuitive, Nancy knew that somehow that snake was telling them to turn around. So she told the people who were driving that she felt they should turn the car around and go back into town. They did go back and met the very people they had missed.

A very dear friend of mine, Alice, has lived in San Diego all of her life and has always felt very close to the sea. Her father was a captain of a fishing boat, and his stories about the birds and animals of the sea entertained her for hours as a child.

One of her favorite places, La Jolla Cove, is a sanctuary for some of her favorite sea creatures, the seal and the sea lion. She and her friends take long walks along the La Jolla coastline often. She always ends up walking out on the sea wall that carves out a small protected cove and beach to see these fascinating animals.

Seals know how to flow with the ever-changing currents. If a seal pops its head into your life, you are possibly being told to learn to go with the flow of life and maintain your balance amid the stormy seas of life.

Seals do not have visible external ears, just small openings. This could represent the inner voice and could be telling us to listen to our inner knowing, and honor our creative, imaginative powers. Seals swim above and below the water, enabling them to experience both the inner and outer worlds. They can teach us how to flow, how to hear, and how to discover the deeper mysteries of our true nature.

All of nature communicates with us on many levels. Blazes of crimson, rose, and orange fill the sky as the sun greets the morning. The trees yawn and stretch to touch the warmth of the sun. The birds fly and sing in joy. What a gift the morning is, a new beginning everyday! Animals join the human watcher slowly walking through the woods as the day begins. The majestic elk stands at the meadow's edge looking across Rocky Mountain National Park, and I wonder what his appearance means for me. Elk are steadfast and persistent. They are sure-footed and graceful. My communion with this animal is power-ful and perfect. We are all connected to the same source of power and Love.

I am learning from the elk to be patient and not judge what I see, to take actions carefully and powerfully. The elk is a sign of beauty, power, dignity, and stamina. They have the power to push through obstacles. When encountering an elk, you might consider in what areas of your life you need to pace yourself in order to be successful.

John had a unique experience around what he called numer-ous sightings of pelicans. He was going through a time in his life that was very difficult for him. As he walked along the coast deep in thought, three pelicans swooped past him. The next day he went to a different spot to walk during his lunch hour trying to unravel a problem that he just couldn't seem to figure out.

He sat down on a bench, and much to his surprise three more pelicans soared majestically past the ocean cliffs and then swooped down to land on a large rock in the ocean right in front of him.

John knew that somehow these pelicans were the key to his turmoil. So he began to do some research around possible meanings for pelicans. As with many symbolic meanings, he found some that didn't really connect with him or his situation. So he sat with himself to discern what these pelicans meant for him. Many of the books suggested that the pelicans represented Christ's sacrifice. The other interpretations, however, appealed to John more, and actually helped him deal with his problem. Pelicans soar majestically past ocean cliffs, reminding us to glide and soar through life instead of giving in to the drudgery we constantly entrap ourselves in. The pelican tells us to remember who we really are, to laugh, soar above our worries, be glad for the adventure we call life. We are reminded that this life is just a side trip on a vast journey.

Sarah had just come back from Chicago and was finally driving up Boulder Canyon at dusk. The canyon is beautiful in the late fall, and suddenly in front of her on this quiet deserted road, a majestic Great Blue Heron soared back and forth in front of her car. She slowed down and watched, almost in an altered state; briefly time stood still as this bird communicated to her silently. She had been pondering a problem all weekend in Chicago, and suddenly she understood she needed to start her own small publishing company.

The next day she asked a friend of hers who was a bird expert all about this giant, graceful bird she had seen. Sarah was told that bird had to be a Great Blue Heron, but they almost never flew up that high in canyons.

Two and half years later after Sarah had quit her "day job" and was writing full time, she had another fascinating experience with the Great Blue Heron. She was driving back from Pagosa Springs early one morning, questioning if she had done the right thing, and if she would be able to make it financially in this new world she was creating for herself. Just at that moment in the early morning sunlight a beautiful Great Blue Heron flew right in front of her car.

The Blue Heron might be a sign of learning to follow our intuition and beginning the journey of self realization. The Blue Heron calls us to delve deeper, to know ourselves and trust our path.

In the fall of 1991 my life felt out of control and overwhelming. I was teaching full time, my oldest daughter had just gone off to spend a semester in Mexico, and I had taken on a second job working three to four hours a night from my home. Several things happened all at once. In the beginning of August, I had a dream that felt more like a vision just before I fell asleep. I saw a large blue X-ray of a woman, and her shoulder was broken. It was so vivid that the next morning I called my friend Dorothe and told her to be careful, because I felt as if this woman was either a friend of hers or somehow very close to her. She said okay. I then promptly forgot about the dream. On September 9th I tripped over our large black lab in the dark and hit a sharp corner of the wall with my shoulder.

The next day as I was looking at the X-ray, it hit me like a ton of bricks that the X-ray (except it wasn't bright blue) was of my shoulder. I was so mad at myself, not only for being stupid, (I should've been more careful), but for not realizing that I was the friend of Dorothe's and should have paid attention because I was warned.

During the same period I had some very strange experiences with wild animals. That same August I was walking the woods behind my home with our two dogs Monty and Bear. Suddenly both dogs stood very still right in front of me, so I stopped and looked around. Through the woods about eight car lengths away under a tree was a huge mountain lion eating a deer.

He looked at us and let out a powerful roar. Basically he just wanted to be left alone to eat. So we walked back the way we came very slowly until it was safe to go home quickly.

Then a week after I had broken my shoulder I was driving up a mountain canyon coming home from work, when a young mountain lion dashed out in front of my car. I swerved and missed her by inches.

By now I am starting to wonder what a mountain lion might symbolize. I had started cutting back on all the things I had committed my time to, including the extra job I was doing from my home at night.

In early October I was driving home late, and much to my surprise a large mountain lion was sitting on a rock next to my driveway. A friend of mine, who believed that animals symbolize things (especially if they come in threes) got me to investigate mountain lion energy. Since I had lived in the mountains since 1976 and had never seen even one mountain lion I agreed to look into it. What I discovered is that the mountain lion represents the balance of body, mind, and spirit. It is a time to stand on your convictions and lead yourself where your heart takes you. So, clearly, the message for me was to start taking time for myself and to get back in balance physically, spiritually, mentally, and emotionally.

Danielle Lin, a well known talk show host, told me about a time in her life when she saw spiders of all shapes and sizes everywhere! This kept happening to the point where other people started to notice that out of the blue, spiders would even dangle in front of her off the ceiling in her office at unexpected times. So one day out of curiosity she stopped in a bookstore that seemed to specialize in shamanistic books, and asked the woman behind the counter if she knew if there were any particular meaning to seeing spiders everywhere. The woman said absolutely, that it was a very good sign. The woman asked her if she was attempting to do anything creative. Danielle replied well, yes, I was writing a wonderful children's book, but people discouraged me so I quit. The woman told her that the spider was the master of creativity and was telling her to use hers. Some meanings for spider are to be creative, to pay attention to opportunities and learn how to weave the fabric of your life in a creative way. Spiders may provide amazing insight and assistance for all of us. Most spiders in the Northern Hemisphere spin webs. One of their messages is to go directly to the center of whatever issue you are dealing with. Be creative, but also be direct. All webs are sticky around the circumference waiting to catch intruders. Spiders tells us to trust our feelings. Look up specific spiders for more specific messages. The Daddy Longlegs for example appear when relationships are deepening. The Tarantula appears when a person is going through a transformation with powerful psychic energy and sensitivity connected to it. Spider tells us to be creative in all our endeavors and follow our instinct in life.

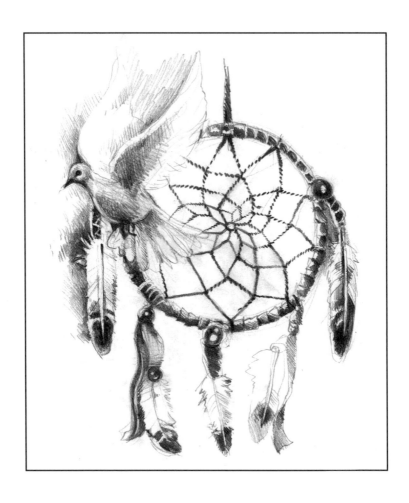

"We are not human beings having a spiritual experience, we are spiritual beings having a human experience."

- Pierre Teilhard de Chardin

Chapter 3

Discovering Past Lives Quickens Synchronicity

It is quite possible that the exploration of past lives triggers a process that helps us understand who we really are. Somehow the search for knowledge brings a response from the Universe as many synchronicities occur. The layers of the material realm become transparent and allow us to see through time. A good example of this process occurred with a young woman named Helen who had taken my friend Dorothe Blackmere's past life regression courses a number of times.

She had many interesting experiences. There was one, however, that not only did she not understand, but didn't seem willing to explore. She had the same experience over and over. She realizes that she is floating in the dome of a beautiful church. The details of the gold mosaic art are very clear. The Pantheonic Christ with his hands outstretched is beautiful and compelling for her. As she told me, she looks down and sees the beautiful marble floor with a rose hue all through it, and then she sees a woman dressed in a blue gown lying on a marble like structure. She realizes with horror that the woman is dead.

Slowly, she goes down closer to see who this person is that all these people are mourning. Women, men, and children are bent down on the marble floor (there weren't any pews in this church) and to her dismay she realizes that the woman is she. Helen had this experience over and over through a three year process, and refused to explore the scene either in the class or on her own.

Dorothe would ask her prodding questions about where she was, and her answer always was the same, "I don't know." Then an opportunity to go to Italy with Dorothe and friends came up, so Helen went because she had never been to Europe and it sounded exciting. They visited all the sights of Rome, enjoying themselves, completely. Then they went to Venice. As soon as they got off the train Helen was energized instantly in a way that was unusual for her; her senses were heightened, and a familiarity with this foreign place was unmistakable.

As they walked towards San Marcos Cathedral her body started to feel strange, almost as if it anticipated a wonderful experience about to happen.

The women stepped through the door of San Marcos' and Helen's whole body started to tingle; she looked down at the floor that had carpet thrown over it to protect the colored marble. It was the rose colored marble she remembered from her regression. She walked to the front of the church and looked up. With amazement she found herself gazing at the beautiful, golden mosaic dome that had become so familiar to her in the dream state. She then looked around and stopped cold; there was a giant rosetta window and she said, "But Dorothe this is exactly like my regression except I know that window was not there."

Weeks later, Helen was helping a student with art history and they were flipping through the book that included the Byzantine period. The next day during her meditation time, on the background of a beautiful indigo screen, a portrait of a woman in a mosaic tiles appeared and she heard a voice say, "PAY ATTENTION." The next week she got the same message and finally looked for mosaic art in the art history book finding the portrait she saw in her meditation.

The woman in the meditation was called Theodora. So Helen went back to Dorothe, had a private session, and was given many details about Theodora's life, much of it very painful. After the private regression Helen was driven to explore more details of this woman's life. Little synchronicities popped up everywhere. As she was looking through books about Theodora's death she was stunned by a line in the book that spoke about the church in Constantinople where she was buried. "The church no longer exists, but if you want to see an exact replica of it except for the large rosetta window go to San Marcos' Cathedral in Venice."

When I interviewed Denise Linn she told me another wonderful story that also happened near Venice, Italy. When Denise was in her twenties she traveled to Italy and went on a gondola ride tour of the islands near Venice. The gondola stopped at St. Francis Island, which Denise had never heard of before. The man who was taking her on the tour said that the monk would show her around the island. The monk greeted her and started to give her a tour. Quickly, as they were walking around, Denise knew what she was going to see (before she actually saw it) and she was having strange deja`vu feelings.

She was startled, as she saw something that looked different from the scenes she was "seeing" in her deja`vu experience. Suddenly, she couldn't contain herself and said, "But that wasn't always here!" The monk looked at her very strangely and said, "No, it is new to the original structure, but it is hundreds of years old."

As she looked at the monk she realized that he was wearing a long, brown, rough fabric robe and pants . . . and so was she! She had just bought three of these brown tunic outfits before leaving the states to go touring in Italy. He had a bowl haircut, and she had gotten her hair cut short in the bowl style that was fashionable at the time, and it looked very much like this Franciscan monk on St. Francis Island hundreds of years before.

Previous to her startling experiences on St. Francis Island, she had some very powerful signs that were purveyors of what was to come. In a city square in Tuscany, she sat next to a pond and all the fish swam towards her. If she moved to another place the fish followed her. People asked her what she was doing to get the fish to all come to her? She was just as surprised as everyone else and said, "I'm not doing anything to get them to come to me." Similarly, wherever she went in Italy, birds began to gather around her, and people would ask what she was doing to attract birds. It seems that the energy from her time as an animal-loving monk had started to emerge even before she had the experiences on St. Francis Island.

When people start to explore their past lives often they will discover connections to people they know in this lifetime. The following story is what happened to Helen. The synchronicities around Helen's research dealing with Theodora led her to other past lives quite coincidentally. As she told me, she stumbled upon a play that was performed in Paris in the late 1800's called Theodora by Sarah Bernhardt. Helen didn't know anything about Sarah Bernhardt, but she felt compelled to read about her life.

Suddenly an eerie feeling came over her that somehow she knew this woman who had acted in a play about her in a past life. So she printed out the materials and called her friend Dorothe. After talking to Dorothe, Helen discovered that she and Sarah Bernhardt had many strange similarities. So she asked Dorothe directly, "Have you ever considered that you might be Sarah?" Dorothe told her she would meditate on it. Several weeks later Helen and Dorothe went to lunch and Sarah came up again. The similarities seemed to etch a clear path through a forest of details. They both have beautiful voices; they both have a son that they were very close to and adore. They both wanted to be a Catholic nun as a child; neither one of them were Catholic; Sarah lost a leg—Dorothe fractured the same leg in two places and had to have advanced surgery to save it; Sarah was a good businesswoman and manager, and so is Dorothe. Sarah and Dorothe share mystical and psychic abilities, and a perfectionist personality when it comes to anything they do, especially in their work. As a mother Dorothe always teased her children and told them to stop acting like Sarah Bernhardt. The details that are similar are too numerous to count. Dorothe has a huge clientele that come from France with their interpreters just to get readings. When Helen asked her what her meditations had shown her, the answer was that yes she and Fred (her son) were together in France as Sarah Bernhardt and son.

Another wonderful story that was told to me came from a close friend, Polly. She told me that one of her favorite synchronicities had to do with her family. Her husband likes to bring back items which their renters leave behind. Usually they are in good or repairable condition, and they use them. One day he brought back a small wooden picture frame with no glass in it. However, he spent money and had glass made for it. They still didn't have a picture for it, and it was placed in an out-of-the-way place in the garage. Their daughter went to the Mall, and uncharacteristically for her, came home with a print of a lovely cottage in the woods done by a French painter. She was going to tack it up on her bedroom wall with thumbtacks. Polly had just that afternoon noticed the picture frame in the garage and brought it in. Voila`! The print was a perfect fit both in size and colors for the frame. In addition, Polly realized it was virtually the same cottage which she had seen many years ago in a past life memory where her husband, daughter, and she had led a wonderful, loving, and simple life. She told me it was a simple memory that came in a meditation over ten years ago. The three of them were living in a rustic cottage somewhere in a French forest. They had simple needs which were always fulfilled. Often they would sit outdoors and eat their modest meals and just enjoy being together and talking. The cottage she saw in her meditation had a thatched roof and sturdy walls. They were very happy there. They enjoyed the sunshine in the glades and the flowers which grew abundantly, but they especially enjoyed being with each other. That was the energy in the print that her daughter picked out "randomly". Independently the three of them had orchestrated a synchronistic experience, and as Polly said as she told me this story, "There are no coincidences!"

Picture green moss, rocky cliffs, seabirds, wild ocean waves crashing powerfully on the rocks, a small town close by a beautiful lighthouse that feels to Sandra like a healing place. There was a gentle giant of a man—her grandfather she thinks. Sandra told me this compelling tale of a lighthouse, lighthouse keeper, and his granddaughter off what she thought was the coast of Scotland. They worked really hard running the lighthouse and the storms were ferocious. She said she felt as if their work saving lives from the sea was very important. One night they pulled a young man from the sea, who appeared to be dead or almost dead, and Sandra said, "I am so upset I put my hands on his head, face, and chest begging for him to live. Light poured from my hands and he started to breathe—we took him inside and he gradually healed, he was sick and weak for a long time. He helped us around the lighthouse to repay us for saving his life. We fell in love." She said, "I recognized his blue eyes from many lifetimes." Now the synchronicity around this experience for Sandra is actually quite extraordinary. She found the exact lighthouse in Scotland as her regression experience; it is on what they call Holy Island and the Tibetan monks take care of it because it is said to be a healing place.

Over the last six years I have attended a number of conferences and workshops with Dr. Brian Weiss. His explanation of how we are all connected touched me deeply. He told us that he likes to think of soul relationships as similar to a large tree with a thousand leaves on it. Those leaves that are on your twig are intimately close to you. You may share experiences, soul experiences, among yourselves. He explained, that there may be three to five leaves on your twig. You are also closely related to leaves on the branch next to yours. They are close to you, but not as close as the leaves on your own twig. As you extend farther out along the tree, you are still related to these other leaves or souls, but not as closely as those in your immediate area. You are all part of one tree and one trunk. You can share experiences. You know each other. But those on your twig are the closest to you through time.

There are many other trees in this beautiful forest that Dr. Weiss describes. Each tree is connected to the others through the root system in the ground. So even though there may be a leaf on a distant tree that seems quite different from you and very far away, you are still connected to that leaf. As he explained, we are connected to all leaves. You are the most closely connected to those on your own tree.

He went on to explain that we probably meet the other souls farther out on your tree in previous lifetimes. They may have been in many different relationships with you, and their interactions may have been brief. One of these souls may have been the beggar in the road to whom you gave a heart's gift, allowing you to extend your compassion to another human being and allowing the recipient to learn about receiving love and help. You and the beggar may have never met again that lifetime, and yet you are part of the drama. Your meetings vary in duration— five minutes, one hour, a day, a month, a decade or more—this is how souls relate. According to Dr. Weiss, relationships are not measured in time but in lessons learned.

He also talks at great length about soul mates and how past life exploration can reveal patterns and reunite loved ones. One particular case he talks about is included in the book *Only Love Is Real* and concerns Elizabeth and Pedro. They were both seeing him as clients to resolve issues. They both had failed or unhappy relationships, and both were dealing with the death of a loved one. Whenever they did their regressions they had lovers or a spouse experience with someone they didn't know this lifetime. After a number of weeks Dr. Weiss realized, as he tells the story in his workshops, that past life scenarios were the same for Pedro and Elizabeth—same time frames, same places, etc. They had never met because they came to his office on different days. So one day he decided to give fate a nudge. He had them scheduled back to back on the same day for appointments. They looked at each other as they went through the waiting room and nothing happened. So Dr. Weiss gave up. Not too much longer after that Pedro had to fly somewhere and Elizabeth had had "one of those days" and missed her flight. So she had to take a different one. They ended up sitting next to each other on the plane, and fell in love and got married. Not only was their meeting filled with meaningful coincidences, but their search for answers to their problems through past life regressions produced a wonderful synchronicity.

"A miracle is never lost. It may touch many
people you have not even met, and
produce undreamed of changes in
situations of which you are not
even aware."

-A Course In Miracles
p.4, text

Chapter 4

Crisis and Death
Accelerate Synchronicity

In the moments of meaningful coincidences are our souls talking to us? Is the language of the soul symbolic and beyond the words of man? Creativity is a gift where men, women, and children learn to treasure the many images and feelings of human existence, but the soul's creativity is connected to a Higher Source that is constantly creating spirals in the galaxies and designs in every snowflake that falls.

It is important for people to not allow themselves to become weighed down by the burdens of the mundane. At a cellular level we are interconnected totally. The statement WE ARE ONE is not symbolic. It is fact. Every thought, feeling, or sensation we experience is felt across the galaxies. As we grow in self discipline, patience, compassion, and unconditional love, we will see synchronicities multiply dramatically. Learning to control our thoughts and words is the most difficult and powerful task we are here to learn.

Many people have had some amazing coincidences and signs show up in their lives during crisis or death situations. I believe this is because we are more open during these times and are paying closer attention to guidance when we need help to cope with difficult circumstances.

Mary's life had become unbearable in a quiet sort of way; silent desperation pressed in around her as she struggled to get out of bed each morning. The death of her grandmother was such a powerful blow to her. Her loneliness overwhelmed her. She was so sad she couldn't even talk about it to anyone. She was five months pregnant with her second child when her grandmother died. She walked along the ocean, sat in quiet churches begging for help from a God who had started to feel very far away from her. For the first time in her life she felt like an orphan. Her father's death was devastating to her, but miraculously her grandmother filled that void with her crystal blue eyes, beautiful Irish smile, and warm hugs that healed the soul.

Then something shifted; Mary's second child was born, and she looked into the eyes of this wonderful little creature who instantly grasped her finger as if to say, "Hello again; I'm here as an answer to your prayers, so smile."

Life seemed to speed up, so Mary sent resumes off to other cities, other states—it was time to move and she knew it. She applied for teaching jobs around the area she lived in, and no matter how close she got, she was turned down. One job she didn't get because she was too qualified. The next job had 1500 applicants and she was in the last round with six other teachers for this highly specialized job, but the previous teacher changed his mind and got his position back.

Mary was devastated and was sure that God had left her out of his Divine Plan. Then through a series of events and after a particularly hard day working at a Howard Johnson's she called a school district in Arizona, and asked to speak to the special ed director.

All of a sudden it felt as if a door opened. The receptionist said, "Dear if you ask for Special Ed Director you will never get through, but if you call back and ask for Dr. Harry Jones I can put you right through to his direct line. Thank you," and she hung up on Mary. So Mary called back and talked to Dr. Jones. He said he would look over her file and get back to her. That was a Thursday morning. Thursday afternoon he called back and said, "Can you be here Tuesday? I have three interviews set up for you." So Mary and her family took a road trip to Arizona. She got offered all three jobs. Her husband told her that it might be hard to sell their condo quickly, and they should at least think about it. They went home, put an ad in the paper, and their condo sold in less than a week. Mary took a job in Flagstaff and it was as if the following two years flowed such that one thing led to another, almost like clockwork.

Periods of major life transitions seem to be fertile ground for an abundance of meaningful coincidences. Personal growth seems not only to facilitate synchronicity, but in turn to be facilitated by it. Synchronistic coincidences are personal events. We are fascinated with synchronicity because of the feeling that each coincidence speaks to us individually. However, sometimes we have to dig deep to find the symbolism in the coincidences that occur.

Anne and Susan have been wonderful friends since kindergarten. They graduated from college together in May, 1994. August of the same year Anne set off on her travels through South America starting in Venezuela. Susan set off to Ecuador to teach English. The two planned to meet up in Ecuador in September or October. Naive about the customs and communication in South America, the two never connected. Come October Susan hadn't heard from Anne and assumed that she had passed through without contacting her. Anne had an address for Susan in Ambato, Ecuador, but it was only a P.O. Box. One day Susan returned from teaching, passed by her P.O. Box, collected her mail, and headed to her apartment three blocks away. She did her usual afternoon tasks at home and was planning on taking her daily nap. Strangely enough, for no apparent reason, she decided to go make copies in preparation for her classes the following day. On the way to the copy shop she thought she would stop by the post office a second time, knowing very well there wouldn't be anything new in her mailbox. She entered the post office, opened the box, and as expected found nothing. She then walked back out the door she had entered two minutes earlier. Across the street she saw a *gringa* and realized it was Anne.

Anne had been sitting on the steps across the street, having been in Ambato since the day before. She had a fever and wasn't feeling well. She didn't have Susan's phone number, or street address, didn't know where she was working, and had no idea where to start looking. Not knowing where to go, she aimlessly wandered to the post office and sat on the steps in front of a nearby building. She was hopelessly trying to figure out how to track Susan down. When they both saw one another they ran towards each other, screaming and crying. They jumped up and down hollering and hooting in the middle of the street for a few minutes, totally unaware of anyone else. They started talking, and didn't stop for the next week until Anne, once again, began to travel.

A number of years ago I had the opportunity to hear Wayne Dyer speak several times. One of his stories has continued to inspire me through the years. He talked about the years he had struggled to come to terms with his father's abandoning his family. He had nightmares, unanswered questions and unresolved pain around this man that he didn't even remember. So at a particularly hard time in his life where basically nothing was going well, from his personal life to his career as a writer and teacher, he got a chance to go to a conference in the South. Years before a cousin had called him to let Wayne know that his father had died in New Orleans. So when the opportunity to go South came up he decided to bring this relationship to some kind of resolution.

He called the hospital where his father had died and found out that his father's body had been shipped to Biloxi, Mississippi. He planned on being in Columbus, Mississippi, which was 200 miles from Biloxi. He wanted his questions answered and thought that somehow by finding his father's grave that maybe he would find peace.

He rented a brand new car in Columbus and was amazed to see the odometer reading was under one mile. When he got into the car he realized that the seat belt was still wrapped up in plastic and tied up under the front seat. So he took out the seat and got the belt out of its plastic wrapper. When he ripped off the plastic, he found a business card tucked inside the buckle. It read Candlelight Inn, Biloxi, Mississippi. He thought that was odd, since the car had not been used yet. He stuck the card in his pocket.

He then drove to Biloxi. When he got there he looked up the cemeteries in the area. There were three. He couldn't get through to the first two he called. An elderly—sounding man answered the phone at the third one. He said he would check to see if Wayne's father was buried there. He found Wayne's father's grave, and Wayne asked if he could visit the grave. The man told him he could and then said, "Your father is buried right next to the grounds of the Candlelight Inn."

Wayne was shaken down to his core as he reached into his pocket and looked at the business card that was in the car 200 miles away. This experience changed Wayne Dyer's life forever. He forgave his father and surrendered all of his pain to the Universe. He said as soon as he did that, his life turned around dramatically for the better.

The first time I took a seminar from Denise Linn she told us an amazing story about a journey that changed her life. At seventeen years old she was shot numerous times by an unknown assailant.

She had searing pain. Slowly the lights began to dim. Then her pain began to subside. The voices in the hospital faded into stillness. She said everything became very dark. Then the black bubble she was in felt as if it burst. A brilliant golden light enveloped her. She said it was so bright that the sun paled in comparison. Light was everywhere. In the light was amazing music. She told us that the music and the light flowed and ebbed together in perfect harmony.

Everything seemed more real than anything she had experienced in this life. Her previous life as Denise on planet earth seemed like a dream or illusion, and the beautiful place was so much more vital and real to her.

One of the amazing and interesting parts of this experience for her was the essence of time. She said all time seemed to flow in a continuous, everlasting "Now." There was no future or past. Completely infused within this world of music and light was love. The love she experienced was infinite and limitless. There was no beginning, no end, just infinite, eternal light.

She experienced being one with everyone and everything. Denise explained to us that our ordinary minds are not big enough to grasp the totality of what she experienced. The only way she could explain it to us was to imagine our life here on earth as a hologram or a reflection of the spiritual dimensions that she encountered when she was shot.

She said she saw a golden river of light in front of her, and if she could make it to the other side of that river she wouldn't have to go back into her broken, injured body. Before she reached the other shore she heard a voice tell her, "You may not stay here. There is something you need to do."

Denise had to heal a badly wounded body. But she now saw everything differently. She saw a radiant light around everything. She could hear the grasses and the trees hum and chant.

She told us that as a result of her near-death experience she now believes that we are each manifestations of pure energy, and that we are all intimately connected. She told us that even if we are not consciously responding to the energy fields around us, we do. Denise was quite clear about our ability to create and manifest the Universe around us.

When I interviewed Denise she was so gracious and comfortable with the topic of synchronicity and signs. She told me that as a result of her near-death experience, she had the realization that there is no separation between thought and creation. During the moments when the doctors thought she was dead, Denise experienced a realm where thought and manifestation were instant. She said, "Here in our earthly reality, there is a time lag between our idea and its manifestation.

However, in that place I entered when I was thought to be dead, creation or manifestation were instant. You think it and it happened."

Denise said that heaven is not a place far away; it is a dimension that coexists with the Here and Now . . . and we all have the ability to tune into this realm, through meditation or through slowing down the mind. She uses the example of a radio that we can tune into many different channels. Each person has inner dials that he or she can use to tune into a multitude of inner dimensions. "Synchronicity starts to happen when you get close to the heavenly dimension. When you tuned into that channel there is less lag time between a thought and the results or manifestation of that desire."

In June 1999, I was sitting in my living room looking out our sliding glass door when suddenly a huge raven landed on the deck. He walked around a little and then stared at me. We looked at each other for over ten minutes. I knew this was a powerful message of some kind, but I wasn't sure exactly what it meant.

The next morning at 5:00 a.m. a doctor from a hospital in San Diego called to tell me that my elderly aunt had been brought in during the night, and that she was critically ill. I made arrangements to fly out the next day. The next morning as I was driving down a canyon road, traffic was held up because of a car accident. When I drove by the accident I somehow knew that the person in the car had died. I looked at the clock; it was 10:40 a.m. As I was preparing to fly to San Diego I learned that my Aunt Helen died exactly at 10:40 a.m. that morning.

As I was flying to San Diego I remembered the raven that had shown up two days before. When I looked raven up I found that it could symbolize taking an inward journey, a big change is coming into your life. My aunt's death started a chain reaction that is still going on even now two years later.

On November 27, 1983 a wonderful young man named Steve was killed in an accident. The synchronicities around Steve's life, and death are too numerous to tell. The connections between Steve's family and the woman who hit him during a November snowstorm are too powerful to be just coincidental. The summer before his death, Steve befriended a little boy who was having a hard time. Steve would go to a junior high school near his home and train for football. He also taught this youngster how to play soccer and kick the ball. Then the fall came, and Steve was too busy to go to the junior high. Apparently the little boy talked about Steve to his family all the time. But they thought he had just made up this big football player to make himself feel better.

However, during that November blizzard the little boy saw Steve's picture in the paper. He couldn't read much yet, so he took the paper to his mother who had been in an accident in the snow and was really upset. Steve had been in the same accident as the little boy's mother.

Another series of synchronicities that occur around Steve remind me of Denise Linn's feather stories. Steve's mother said that for some reason they started connecting finding pennies with Steve. He had always saved pennies, and there was a huge jar of pennies in his room. They started finding pennies everywhere, and in some very strange places. They felt that Steve was communicating with them somehow.

I was Steve's teacher, and it was very hard on me when he died. Steve's mother told me about the pennies, and much to my surprise I started noticing at particularly hard times in my life I would find one single penny in places that I knew there weren't any pennies just moments before. There was one day that stands out as being quite difficult, and I went to get into my 4 Runner, and on the running board was a penny. I was so cranky I just left it there and drove up my winding mountain road home. Much to my surprise when I got out of the car twenty-five miles later the penny was still there. I had to start laughing because Steve was pretty stubborn, and I knew he was not only telling me everything would be okay, but also he wanted me to pay attention and lighten up.

Suzanne, of NAPRA (Networking Alternatives for Publishers, Retailers & Artists) told me a wonderful story about the experiences she had around her family's illnesses and death. Every time she went up to her family's property a large eagle would circle above her, spiraling towards the sky. She had her first eagle sighting during her father's burial. She was so sad, but then suddenly a huge, majestic eagle soared up above her father's grave and circled around several times. She said that somehow she knew that it was a sign that her father was okay.

Deb Jordan, owner of the Phoenix Phyre Book Store in Encintas, told me an amazing story. From the time her father was five years old, all he ever wanted was to be a Marine. When she was four years old, her father was sent into a little known region that was beginning to experience Communist hostility—it was called VietNam. He went in as an observer/advisor reporting back to the Pentagon to determine whether U.S. Military intervention would someday be necessary. Almost a year after he left, her sister, then seven, had a dream. Almost inconsolable, she told her mother he was dead. He had been shot in the head with a bullet. Her mother assured her this was not true and read her father's letters to her, let her listen to tape recordings her father sent from Okinawa. Her sister could not be convinced. Finally in desperation, her father came home on emergency leave. It was a few weeks before Christmas. He was able to stay for two weeks. Her sister was consoled, and he returned to Vietnam for his final two months of tour. It was a Saturday in February, a package came which contained the most beautiful matching oriental jewelry boxes for her and her sister. They were intricately detailed, with many drawers and compartments. When the girls lifted the top, the song "Sayonara" played, Japanese for goodbye.

That night, after their mother put them to bed, she sat in the living room reading, then was startled by her father's voice. Just his voice. He said he had to leave, but he loved her and the girls, and that everything would be all right. Her mother knew he was dead. The following morning she hurried her daughters through their morning routine, dressed them, and scurried them off to stay with the neighbor. Deb remembered sitting on the front porch playing Go-Fish when a group of men came to her home. She was so excited she leaped from the porch and began running towards the house. She tripped and scraped both of her knees, and a kindly reporter scooped her up and carried her back to the neighbors to bandage her skinned knees. The Colonel, Chaplain, and reporter entered her house and told her mother what she already knew. Three weeks before he would return home, and two weeks before his 33rd birthday, her father entered enemy territory. The Battalion was ambushed and her father died. A mortar fragment hit his head. Her sister's dream had come true, and their jewelry boxes from their father said goodbye.

Ed Rubenstein, author and psychologist told me a story of how synchronicity altered the course of his life. When he was a teenager he had some wake-up calls that he was not listening to. This avoidance led him to a near-death experience that resulted when a vehicle going sixty mph ran into his car door. He had a life review, his whole life flashed before his eyes. The gift of the impact from that vehicle woke him up from what he described as a deep slumber. The right books appeared at the right time to support his spiritual yearning. He began to desire deeper spiritual experience. He applied to the Peace Corps, and the next thing he knew he was in Katmandu, Nepal. He organized the construction of gravity flow water systems in villages where up to fifty percent of the children died from dehydration.

Through a continued combination of synchronistic events, he ended up meeting a yogic monk who became his meditation teacher and supported him on his spiritual journey. That happened in 1975 and since that time, he can see how a series of synchronistic events served as pivot points which influenced the unfolding direction of his life. This includes events that led to the meeting of his wife, shifts that led him to a different direction on his spiritual path, and synchronicities which facilitated his becoming open to new paradigms. These teachings and inner experiences have supported him in being more aligned with his soul and have allowed him to be of greater service to the clients he works with.

The following story seems to be filled with what Angeles Arrien calls grace. Tom and his brother were raised by divorced parents. Their father always carried a photograph of a young boy in his wallet. As children, when they asked about the photograph, they were told it was a neighbor's child that the father had been close to. When they reached young adulthood, their father sat them down and told them that the boy in the photograph was in actuality their brother. The father had been previously married and had had a son, Patrick. As a toddler, Patrick had wandered into a lake and drowned. That was the extent of the story and further inquiry was brushed off.

The idea of having an unknown brother haunted Tom. In his mid thirties, he was planning a business trip to the East Coast and decided to see what information he could find. Always the keeper of family memorabilia, Tom had a very old address book of his grandmothers. Looking in it, he found his father's name with what must have been his first wife, listing a street and small town in Connecticut. During his business trip, he rented a car and drove to the small town. Having no idea where he was going, he just drove aimlessly. He followed a small dirt road to a small lake. Sitting stunned, he knew within his heart that this was where his brother had died, some forty years earlier. As he sat in the rented car, an old man came walking down the path eyeing him suspiciously. He rolled down the window and greeted the man trying to be as friendly as possible since he was a bit out of place. The old man asked what he was doing and he simply said; "I think my brother died in this lake forty years ago." A bit taken aback the old man said, "I was there when your father pulled the baby from the lake." First thinking okay we have a nut here, Tom then realized he never said the child was a baby.

The old man went on to tell the story. The young couple, Tom's father and wife, lived in the small house set off from the lake. One afternoon their two year old toddler followed a dog down to the lake. The mother did not know he had wandered from the house. He fell into the lake and drowned. His father upon coming home began looking for the toddler. He found him in the lake and pulled him out. He was already dead. The old man said the young couple moved just a few days later and he never saw them again.

Tom asked if he, by chance, knew where the baby was buried. The old man said there was a cemetery up the road a bit and around the bend. Thanking the old man, Tom drove to the cemetery. He walked among all the tombstones, but found no marker for Patrick. As he was about to leave, he looked to the top of the hill and saw a low flat area. Climbing the hill, he found small flat markers for the children who had died. At the far end covered in vines was Patrick's grave. Due to the coincidence of the old man on the path, Tom found his brother.

In November, 1999 I went to a Body and Soul Conference in San Francisco. I had just done a book signing at the East West Bookstore and planned to drive down to Southern California on Monday to finish organizing the storage unit that my aunt had left. I was really looking forward to this conference and listening Brian Weiss and James Van Praagh.

As I sat in the large hall with over three hundred other people, James Van Praagh had just completed an amazing meditation that made me tingle all over. He had just finished four readings and was going to do one more, then end the session. To this day I can't tell you my amazement when I realized he was motioning for me to stand up. He was rubbing his forehead and saying that a man named John wanted to talk to me, and that he was my father who had been dead for over thirty years. He went on to describe situations and people in my life with amazing accuracy. He said that it was important for my father to let me know he was all right and proud of me and my children. Then my grandmother and aunt, who had just died, came through with very powerful messages. I was overwhelmed.

The following Monday I drove down the coast. That week I cleaned out the storage unit my aunt had kept with things that had been saved for over fifty years from my family and their history. It was very hard to go through it. I came upon a small suitcase that was filled with cards and letters of my fathers before he died thirty years before. Then I found letters from my mother that my father had saved that I had never seen. All of this created a very powerful transformation for me, and the timing of what I call a phone call from my family was beyond the realm of coincidence.

Like my family, Sam Houston came from a long line of fighting Irish. When he was fourteen, his father died and his mother moved her family of nine boys to Tennessee. Sam was large, strong-willed, and rebellious. He ran away and joined a tribe of Cherokee Indians, he stayed with them for three years. He went on to open a school, join the army, and fight under General Andrew Jackson. He recovered from supposedly fatal wounds and, even through amazing hardships seemed to have a charmed life. He studied law and went on to be elected to Congress and then Governor of Tennessee. He married Eliza Allen. The marriage was brief, for his wife left him for another man and Sam could not bear to lose his love. So he resigned from the governorship and took a boat toward the wilderness, not caring about the future of his life. He was so depressed as the story goes that he seriously contemplated suicide. Then, at that very moment a giant eagle swooped close to the deck, then flew screaming into the sunset. Sam Houston because of his background with the Indians, took this as a sign that the eagle's flight indicated a future for him in the West. He finally ended up in Texas where the rest of his story is history.

Raleigh Pinskey, publicist and author told me a wonderful story of how she reluctantly wrote her first book. She was in public relations dealing with music clients in New York City. She liked her life and her lifestyle. A soap opera star asked her to work with him while he wrote his first book. The learning curve for her was steep, because publicity in the book world was a little different from the music world. She then at the same time saw a very accurate psychic who told her she would be writing books of her own as part of her future and destiny. Well, Raleigh fought the whole idea of writing books until finally one thing led to another and now she has a number of wonderful books: *101 Ways To Write Foolproof Media Releases, 101 Ways To Get On Talk Shows, The Zen of Hype* and *101 Ways To Promote Yourself.* She has learned to concentrate when things start to happen that appear synchronistic or symbolic and ask her angels and guides for guidance and clarity.

According to Marilyn Ross, synchronicity can wear many hats and come camouflaged in different costumes. When she and her partner in life, Tom moved from San Diego to a small Colorado town in 1980 she went into culture shock after living her life in California. She was very lonely and missed her family and friends in San Diego. She wasn't sure she was going to be able to handle her new way of life without all the people she loved around her. Something quite miraculous started happening. In their business, they help professionals self publish their books through their company, About Books, Inc. One day a gentleman called and said he and his wife wanted to come from South Carolina and have a meeting with them after hearing one of their speeches. A week later this delightful couple was in their offices making arrangements to do his book, and they ended up buying property there the same weekend.

Little did they know then how much this couple would come to mean to them. A friendship that has grown and ripened beyond her wildest dreams was born. The Blacks moved to Buena Vista and consider the Rosses their best friends. Marilyn has many wonderful stories around people who worked with them and then moved to the area and live by them. The Universe works in miraculous ways and helped her have new friends near where she lives now.

In 1996 Tom and Marilyn decided to start a nonprofit organization as a way to give something back to an industry that had been good to them. SPAN (the Small Publishers Association of North America) now has over 1300 members all across the U.S. and Canada. According to Marilyn these are the most amazing people; they get letters, phone calls, and e-mails of appreciation daily. And what is especially satisfying to Marilyn is that a few of the members have chosen to become deeply involved, thus giving her the opportunity to really know them well. "The synchronicities around some of the members have been intriguing and powerful, especially between Sandra, Patricia, Merry and myself. We all live in different parts of the country, but we have become very close friends and help each other out constantly."

Gloria, an amazing artist told me how four years ago she felt unjustly forced out her job that she wanted in New York City. She sought refuge in a cabin she had purchased several years before which was snowbound in winter so seeking regular employment was prohibitive. Simultaneously, she expressed a desire to illustrate a book by an author searching for a publisher, and within the year she had a contract. She is now on a completely more satisfying career path as an artist and illustrator.

Paola Harris was a journalist working in Rome for a magazine and doing stories on the UFO phenomenon when her office encouraged her to attend the fiftieth anniversary of the Roswell incident that was to be a media event because of the debut of Col. Philip Corso's book *The Day After Roswell*. Numerous synchronicities occurred during this trip. It started with Paola having no transportation from Boulder, Colorado, where she lives in the summer to Roswell, New Mexico (1200 miles roundtrip), to no place to stay once she got there. This was a huge media event and every hotel had been booked months in advance. Out of the blue she was offered a ride with Richard Sigismond (local Boulderite and world renowned UFO specialist). When she got there she opened the telephone book at "random" and found an empty room at the Sallyport Inn for the exact three days she would be there. Her next obstacle was finding a way to talk to Colonel Corso. He was surrounded by agents and security people, so her chances of getting an interview were really pretty slim.

As Paola put it, "Quite by accident I returned to my hotel and as I was walking out of my room, I saw Colonel Corso coming down the hall towards me. He saw me and said, "I need to talk to you, young lady about the electro-magnetic pillars in the Roswell Desert in 1947." She then realized with a shock he was entering the room right next to hers. As the story continues Paola became quite close to the Corso family and wrote the preface to the Italian version of *The Day After Roswell.*

As Paola was preparing to write about the first incident, she received a telephone call from a cameraman who was working on another film project but wanted to follow up on a past shoot they had done in Tivoli together while interviewing witnesses and contactees on the UFO phenomenon. They had not been able to fit in the follow-up footage this time around, but just by chance (Paola's words) she asked him what was the current film he was working on. He responded by saying that they were filming the Pope, the Vatican area and Saint Peter's for a documentary called *"Elvis and the Pope."* The film concerned the selling of religious articles, Elvis paraphernalia, and the marketing of an image.

Paola was startled; the story she was about to write and send to me was about her synchronistic experience around Elvis. She told the man that she had been an Elvis groupie in 1975–1976 and could tell them many fascinating stories. So they interviewed her, and the program will air on American television.

She had been an Elvis fan since her teenage years. When she saw him in 1976 in person, she was able to talk to him because she gave him a picture of himself as a young man that he loved. He in turn gave her the white scarf he was wearing around his neck. Paola was devastated when he died in August 1977. A year after his death she went with some friends to his grave.

She had had a strange dream before she went. There were two people she had never met. She went up a long driveway and entered a sacred place like a sanctuary. It had yellow gold carpeting and wood paneling on the walls. Elvis was hugging a lady with gray curly hair and (in the dream) she interrupted him asking for his autograph. Annoyed, he said, "Wait a minute girl" and hugged a tall thin gentleman next to the lady almost crushing him in a bear hug. He told the gentleman, "You are doing a good job, Al" (or at least it was something like Al). Then he turned to Paola and said the concerts are over you must walk The Land of the Lord. He then sat down and drew his arms around his stomach in pain. Paola woke up crying and she was surprised by his religious fervor. She wrote this dream down and forgot about it. When she and her friends got to Memphis about 1600 people were there too. She got invited to go to church with Elvis's cousin Donna Early and her mother Mrs. Pritchard because they accidentally bumped into her with their car. Somehow the church felt familiar to her but she couldn't remember why. As she opened the hymnbook she saw the words WALK THE LAND OF THE LORD. It was a hymn and everything in her dream was there including the woman with the curly gray hair. So after the service Paola told them about the strange dream she had. When she described the man, it was the precise description of Mrs. Pritchard's husband Earl who at that time was the gardener caretaker at Graceland and who was quite despondent over Elvis's death. Donna and her mother had Paola give her message to Earl in person, he was definitely the man in the dream and the message clearly helped him deal with Elvis's death.

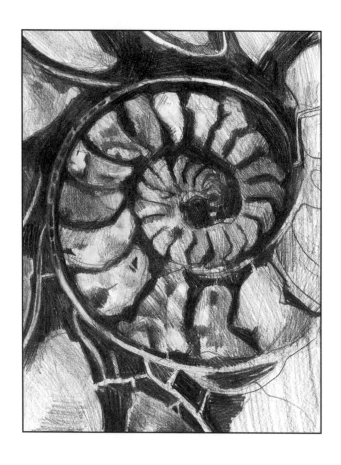

"This is the most profound spiritual truth I
know: that even when we're most sure that
love can't conquer all, it seems to anyway."

- Anne Lamott

Chapter 5

Harmonious Universe

The natural essence of the Universe is perfect harmony. Spirals, labyrinths, numbers, and other symbols create a myriad of intersecting landscapes for us to investigate. There is no point where God begins or ends. Our lives are intimately connected to everything. There are those who hope to dissect the parts and thereby understand the whole. Thus mystics and scientists travel down different roads, but their destination is the same.

The majesty of the Universe is beyond our minds. The symphony of the Cosmos is beautiful and harmonious. Sunflowers grow, in spite of the weeds, reaching for the sun. Hummingbirds remind us to taste and enjoy the sweet nectar of life. Coyotes trot into our lives to help us laugh, and be creative in our undertakings.

Spirals and labyrinths connect us to our souls, and remind us who we really are. Numbers throughout the ages guide us to the mysteries of the Universe as we learn their codes. Cooperation and harmony is the way of Nature. Greed and discord is not natural. Our lives are designed to follow a plan that promotes growth, joy, and harmony. Anything that doesn't fit in that category is a waste of time.

Our choices are filled with patterns; life is cyclical just as the seasons come and go in rebirth, renewal, and apparent death. The vast Universe is filled with song, color and dimensions. To limit our vision with fear, guilt, or quiet despair slows down our growth. We are all here to expand, sing and rejoice. Violence, anger, greed and jealousy creates imbalance in our lives. Depression is a sign that we need to listen to the song of our souls.

Frank Joseph told me that synchronicities instill compassion for all living things, because they help us to see that each one is an important piece in the growing mosaic of creation, which is an unfinished artwork that would be diminished by the loss of a single fragment.

The symbolic world is the language of the Universe. Thus words often do not convey the essence of truth. Our perceptions create our inner stories, which in turn create the directions of our lives. Spirals, triangles, circles, squares, and crosses evoke feelings of connectedness that seems universal among humans throughout history. Different cultures, arts, and designs tell us their stories through the symbolic world. Fractals intrigue many who then discover a new aesthetic blending of art, science, and nature.

One of the reasons that our systems and institutions are struggling on this planet is because people are evolving to new levels. They need different perspectives, different and more open techniques to discover the world around them. They deserve to be validated as human beings. Their stories are weaving the 21st Century's history, and as a society we must make the shift necessary to help our searching minds and hearts.

Unfortunately, depression is rampant on this planet. Technology has become more valuable than soul to many. A major shift is occurring, not just on our planet but within the human psyche. Mysteries are cropping up all over the place. Questions are being asked and answers are being sought. For centuries science has tried to be disconnected from the spiritual realm.

However, Dr. Candace Pert, author of *Molecules of Emotion* has discovered that our cells respond to our emotions everywhere in the body. Now Dr. Pert is one of many scientists who are exploring the mind, body, and spirit connection. Her research has shown clearly that cells at the most minute levels communicate with each other. They vibrate to different frequencies and will start to vibrate together over a period of time, depending on the actions of other cells around them. The cells seem to have intelligence at all levels within the body.

According to Frank Joseph, the human microcosm and the cosmic macrocosm intersect at a special point in time to become one for an immeasurable instant. He believes that synchronicity leads us to the conclusion that we personally, as well as every cell in our body, are connected to and part of the Universal Purpose.

The symbolic world is a rich resource for us. We have symbolic systems that have been used throughout history. Although many look upon tarot decks, runes, and the I Ching with suspicion, these symbolic systems are tools to allow us to use and develop our own intuition. Prayer beads, prayer wheels, mantras, rosary beads, crosses, and mandalas are all tools to allow us to connect with our spiritual essence.

Our challenge is to learn to interpret and discern truth. No culture, religion, or society has exclusive rights to truth. We are here to discover who we really are, why we are here, and where we are going. In general the old world view considered violence a viable solution to all problems. Slowly, people are learning new ways of dealing with problems. If, as scientists and mystics tell us, we are all connected, then to hurt another being is in essence hurting ourselves as a whole.

We have to learn different skills and seek different solutions for our problems. Violence is not evil; violence is stupid. What most people call evil is really intense stupidity. If we all knew the truth about our Universe and world we would never consciously hurt another person or being.

Our connections go beyond the human form. There are powerful and intricate patterns forming constantly throughout the cosmos. We are connected to every cell and molecule that exists. Spirals, shapes, or labyrinths intertwine throughout the Universe, creating all that we see, hear, or experience. Sound, sacred geometry, cells, patterns in trees, leaves, flowers, snails, and seashells all speak to us in ways that the conscious intellect does not usually understand.

People respond to different shapes depending on what is going on in their lives. A friend of mine whose life has been in turmoil for years is drawn to the square. She says it feels safe, secure, and solid to her. The spiral isn't interesting to her and it doesn't draw her attention at this time in her life.

Cellular patterns, solar systems, and waves of music all create patterns that respond to our living breathing Universe. I have attended a number of workshops given by Angeles Arrien throughout the past six years. She has done extensive work on symbols. In her workshops she used to do a shape test to help the participants figure out where they were right then, what their strengths were, where they thought they were, what their motivation is, and what old or unfinished business they have to deal with. Angeles has also written a wonderful book that includes this test and gives us directions and explanations for their use. *SIGNS OF LIFE, The Five Universal Shapes and How to Use Them* is a wonderful resource that I would recommend for anyone interested in self discovery.

Mandala, the Sanskrit word for circle, is a concrete symbol of its creator's expression of sacred center. They are meant to draw the viewer and the creator into an encounter with active sources of energy. They are used as a healing and transforming tool in Native American sand painting, Hindu and Tibetan rituals, guided imagery in music, and modern therapy. Labyrinths, which are circular walkways created from sacred geometry occur all over the world from Chartre Cathedral to hand held varieties. Walking them allows you to become part of an integrating mandala that leads a person to universal unity and wholeness.

Our ancestors used labyrinth shapes through the ages. The labyrinth connects us to our souls. It offers us space to listen to ourselves. It can be slow and contemplative experience, or fast and energizing; it can help us shed layers of emotions and unravel a problem; or it can stimulate the mind and offer inspiration. Recently labyrinths have become popular again. They are being restored and replicas of them made across the globe. We can also see the shape of the labyrinth all around us in the spiraling and turning of nature. Spider webs, the swirl of our thumb prints, and the tumultuous clouds of a hurricane all speak to us at a subconscious level.

Furthermore stars, crescent moons, and spirals all symbolize powerful energies and emotions. These symbols have been around long before civilized man. The Etruscans, the Greeks, the Mayans, the Egyptians and the Celtic people all felt the power and importance of these symbols and their connection to the Universe.

Quantum physics is proving that we are all deeply interconnected at a cellular level. The ancients sensed this and developed intricate codes and rituals to help all of us develop and grow. Daily troubles are part of the human experience, but they can wear us down if that is all we focus on.

The power of focus is important, no matter what your life style or age. Energy follows thought; what you think is what you get; so the most important step in any process is the control of your own mind, thoughts, hopes and wishes. Many of the ancient symbolic systems were developed to help initiates of the mystery schools focus and develop their intuition. Some examples of these systems occur in the runes and the I Ching. It is important when using any system to develop a meditative way of being and allow Spirit to guide you along your path. Asking for help is useless if you do not sit quietly and listen to the answers.

However, listening can be hard work. Developing self discipline and paying attention to ourselves, to the vital signs that blip across the screen of our lives in forms such as dreams, intuitions, feedback and longings, will help us know what our souls are communicating to us. The practice of listening will tell us what's true and what's not, when to proceed and when to postpone, whom to trust and whom not to trust, which direction to take at the crossroad and what's right for us and our lives.

The spiral is a highly complex symbol. It has been used since paleolithic times and appears in pre dynastic Egypt, Crete, Mycene, Mesopotamia, India, China, Japan, pre-Columbian America, Europe, Scandinavia and Britain. It variously represents both solar and lunar power, air, the waters, rolling thunder and lightning, growth, expansion, energy vortexes, the creative force, winding and unwinding birth and death, fertility, Chinese dragon, the ear, the tentacles of the octopus and even kundalini energy.

It stands for the repetitive rhythm of life, the cyclical nature of evolution and the permanence of being beneath the flux of movement. The spiral also can symbolize the soul's journey after death.

Jacquelyn Small told me an interesting story. One evening she was to give a short talk to a group in Austin, Texas. She wanted to talk about infinity. Her friend told her that she thought that was too deep a subject for the group she would be addressing. As she stepped out of the car to go to the meeting, she noticed a string lying near her foot in the shape of an infinity sign—a sideways figure eight. She spoke on infinity that evening, and it was a profoundly meaningful experience for several people. She was really glad that she followed her instinct that night.

People dealing with spiral energy need variety, change and novelty. They hate routine and are capable of doing multiple tasks well. They are learning to grow and develop at different levels of awareness. Oftentimes when we are involved in a great deal of change we need creativity to handle life's challenges with integrity.

According to Angeles Arrien there are stories in all cultures around the life-renewing potential of the spiral. Rumplestilskn, the Native American tales of Spider Woman, the European tales around Arachne, and stories of Arianski (Spider Man) are just a few examples.

Another symbol that is considered to have universal meanings is the circle. The circle stands for unity and wholeness. A series of circles, one inside the other, is commonly found as a symbol of the cosmos. Lacking beginning or end, a circle represents infinity, perfection, and the eternal. Often the circle is used as a symbol of God. The Buddhist and Hindu wheel of life is a circle that symbolizes the constant cycle of change. Also, circles were considered harmonious and protective, especially in the Celtic world.

In Zen, the empty circle represents enlightenment. The circle surrounding the cross is the union of male and female principles of life, both human and divine. Carl Jung saw the circle as a symbol of the psyche and the self. Angeles Arrien says that people involved in the process of wholeness are drawn to the circle. She feels that it is really important to give those people enough space, because it is vital not only for their growth but for their process of individuation.

The cross is a universal symbol from ancient times. The cross represented the Tree of Life and the Tree of Nourishment; it also can be a symbol of the archetypal person, capable of infinite and harmonious expansion on the horizontal and vertical planes. Literature and mythology is filled with stories of the shared journey; the cross also represents this journey. Some powerful examples of this shared journey are Isis and Osiris, Shiva and Shakti, Tristan and Isolde, King Arthur and Guinevere.

The cross universally stands for integration and relationship issues. Balance, synthesis, and partnership is really important to the person involved with the cross as a symbol. The need for connections is very powerful while a person is dealing with these issues that the cross represents according to Angeles Arrien.

We have been fascinated with the triangle throughout time. It is connected to the pyramids and arrowheads. The underlying symbolism of the triangle is visions, dreams, goals, revelation, and self discovery. It is an active symbol for spirit and reaching for higher realms. This symbol can also stand for protection and a time of integration. In Christianity it stands for the Holy Trinity. Two triangles, one in the normal position and one inverted superimposed on the first form, a six pointed star. This star is known as the Star of David or Solomon's Seal, and it is the symbol for the human soul.

The square is important to those who are ready to build, to manifest a project or idea, or take action on a plan. Consistency, accountability and finishing something is very important for people connecting to the square. They value integrity and want results.

Numbers are also very significant in the symbolic world. Julie, an artist by trade, has had many experiences. Here is one that she shared with me around the number eight and meaningful coincidences that occurred. For a few years she lived in a small seaside community in a quaint wood frame cottage nestled between Eighth street and Little Orphan Alley. Her address number added up to eight. Her father became seriously ill during that time and she spent her life at that time painting and taking care of her father. After he died she saw an astrologer who asked her if her father had passed recently. She told Julie that Saturn had just moved into her eighth (deals with death among other things) house in her chart days prior to her fathers death. So 8th street, Little Orphan Alley and her astrology chart all spoke to her about the loss of her father.

Over the last five years I began to notice numbers showing up in my life, over and over. It seemed so strange, but I couldn't ignore waking up every night at 4:44 for weeks; or seeing 11:11 or 5:55 on almost everything from clocks to buildings. Many of the people I interviewed had similar experiences around numbers, so I started investigating the meanings and history of numbers.

Pythagorus, father of mathematics, the great mystic and philosopher, and musical theorist taught his students that figures were for measurement, (how much, how far, how heavy) and that numbers represented spiritual qualities and processes. The meanings of figures are exoteric, or easily understood, and that numbers are esoteric, with hidden meanings. He felt that the numbers one through nine symbolized the underlying structure and orderly progression of all life, and the number ten completed the cycle.

Esoteric numerology is the art and science of understanding the spiritual significance and orderly progression of all manifestation. Every name or word vibrates to a number, and every number has its inner meaning. Pythagorus was born around 582 B.C. on the Greek Island of Samos in the Aegean Sea. He traveled to Egypt, where he was initiated into certain mathematical doctrines. He is also reported to have studied with Zoroaster, the Persian sage, and to have learned the Kabbalah in Judea. In fact the science of numbers he taught was based on Kabbalistic principles.

He settled in Crotona in southern Italy and established a school of the mysteries. His students had to know arithmetic, music, astronomy, and geometry before they could proceed into the Pythagorean mysteries. The Greeks thought the Golden Mean was the divine ratio. They considered its ratio to be the most beautiful fit in nature, physically, aesthetically, even morally. So they took it from nature and put it into their art and philosophy. It appears in their painting, architecture, sculpture, and music. These proportions are what we call classical.

Kepler called the Golden Mean the divine proportion. This ratio is found everywhere, for example in the center of a sunflower where the seed pad shows us a fifteen-point mandala. The wild rose shows it in five opened petals. The apple blossom takes this same ratio and actually turns it into the five point star that is found in the cross-section of an apple.

Fractals occur in all of nature. They can be described as the science of patterned chaos, which charts patterns that recur on scales small and large in the timing and spacing of energy and matter. In patterned chaos we can predict an overall pattern, but it is also chaotic chance because we cannot specify any exact point of its next occurrence. We can determine its general form but not its exact contents. Science tells us that patterned chaos must include the following: cycling that repeats with continual light variation, scaling that fits one level into another, universal applicability and order in the midst of apparent disorder. At a Body and Soul Conference in Boulder, Colorado several years ago I listened to a wonderful story by Deepak Chopra as he explained the chaos theory in human terms. He asked us to imagine Grand Central Station, with people running and scurrying everywhere to catch trains, and then a call goes out over the loudspeaker that the train on track nine has been changed to track two, etc. On the surface we would see what appears to be random chaos, and yet there is order and specific purpose to the people running all over the place and changing their patterns suddenly. We just don't have the perspective to see the overall controls in the Universe, so we think everything is random and chaotic, when in actuality it is perfect just the way it is.

According to Candace Powers, a numerologist, 444 is a karmic number and definitely connected to "spirit trying to contact you or angels nudging you to move to the next level or a different direction." Frank Joseph, author of *Synchronicity And You* said there were historic references connecting four to the Christ Child. Arielle Ford told me she and her husband both started to see 444 everywhere when they first met and started their relationship. Many people told me that it meant that angels are talking to you.

Gayle, owner of Transitions Bookplace in Chicago, told me she sees 11:11 all the time, especially if she is about to have contact with a very special lady that has been a supportive and helpful friend to her for years. Astrologer Susan Miller has had many unusual experiences with numbers. One of her stories occurred around what she felt was a magical address for her. She got her first job at *Life Magazine,* published her first book, started her first web site, and has had her first textbook published all at 1271 Avenue of the Americas at different times in her life. She also told me that 47 was an amazingly lucky number for her. When she gets a phone number to call back and it has 47 in it, she knows it will be good for her somehow. Interestingly enough, after the interview I realized that 1271 and 47 both add up to the number 11. Pythagorus said, "Eleven is the number of a cycle of new beginnings." In numerology eleven is known to have the power to change environments, to create new conditions, and build new lives, all in harmony with the Divine.

Eleven is considered the number of Light. It represents the hidden Knower. The number eleven stands for the self and the Christ Self. Individuals who are connected to the eleven vibration on any level must find Light and share it with all they come in contact with, sharing a new dawn of awareness. Nancy Lee, popular talk show host, had many experiences with reoccurring numbers, especially 444, 8, 11:11 and 10. Last fall she was able to take a ten day trip during the tenth month, October, for $199.00 which adds up to 10. This trip is one that she had wanted to go on for a long time. It was a sacred site tour where she was able to find a deep part of herself and connect to her spiritual self. It had a powerful impact on her.

Danielle Lin, also a well-known talk show host, used to see 444 all the time. More recently she now is waking up at 4:23 a.m. Because of her background as a numerologist she added the numbers together and got nine. She said for her she felt the nine was about transformation. And in fact her life was transforming dramatically. She felt she was moving towards more creativity and healing in her life at this time.

Haley Garwood, historical fiction author, told me this story regarding numbers. "I was born 04/40. At one point this number was coming up every time I turned around. My mother's license number was 440; my literary agent's address was 440; the last 4 digits of her phone number was 0440; my current special boyfriend's Jersey number , from many years ago was 44," she also had a number of strange coincidences around birth dates and phone numbers that seemed too connected to be as she put it "random."

Joye, a good friend of mine, has had numerous experiences that could be considered extraordinary. When she arrived in Boulder she was issued a new license plate for her car. It was ML 56. ML were the initials of her namesake and 56 is the middle portion of her social security number. She felt she had personalized license plates. If you multiply the month and day of time she was born you come up with 56, which by the way adds up to eleven. She also has always considered her lucky number four. Her new license plate is 4404. She often wins prizes or contests with the number four somehow involved.

It seems that science, history, art, and nature all point to a very organized and symmetrical universe. In ancient Egypt and Greece there occurred an extensive use of what early 20th Century geometrician Jay Hambridge dubbed "dynamic symmetry." Both Egyptian and Greek sacred objects and buildings have geometries based upon the divisions of space attained by root rectangles and their derivatives.

The Fibonacci Series, named after Leonardo Fibonacci, revolutionized mathematics. This numerical series is recognized as a principle inherent in the structure of the universe. The arrangement of leaves on a plant, the pads on a cat's foot, the spirals encountered in pine cones and pineapples are all governed by the Fibonacci series.

Our solar system and the Universe are seething with invisible energies that work in mysterious but rhythmical ways. Numbers are powerful symbols and signs that communicate their messages. Our job is to quiet our minds and thoughts enough to hear and understand what is being communicated to us.

Frank Joseph told me that synchronicity is a direct experience with God. In any event that is connected with synchronicity, God begins to identify Him/Herself as the sum total of every item comprising the whole universe. Dr. Joseph continued by saying, "Every particle of creation is a living detail of the Creator, whose complete identity is expressed only in the totality of existence."

As I was writing this book the concept of the morphic resonance field came up over and over again. The story of the Hundredth Monkey as a concept was raised on numerous occasions by people who had no relationship with each other. The question to be posed and responded to is, "Will humanity make a quantum leap into consciousness gravitating towards unconditional love, forgiveness, nonjudgment and harmony?" I do believe we are heading in that direction, and that each person needs to consciously monitor their thoughts, actions and direction. I believe we cause ripples that are felt across the universe and each one of us is adding power to the growth of our species, especially by paying attention to synchronicities, signs, and symbols.

Synchronicity, Signs and Symbol Journal

The following pages are meant to help you get started on your journal, with some definitions to help you along your path. There are many wonderful books on the subject of symbolic understanding. It is very important, however, for you to learn to sit with yourself quietly everyday and discover what a certain sign or occurrence means for you. You are the ultimate authority on your life. Learn to pay attention to what the Universe is whispering to you.

A daily meditation of some form is a good way to start noticing the signs and symbols in your life. The Open Heart Meditation is one that I highly recommend. Become a center of love and kindness in this moment. The world will have a nucleus of love that it didn't have the moment before. Center yourself either sitting or lying down quietly. Place your hands on your solar plexus with your fingers together. Breathe deeply. Take several deep breaths. Allow images of kindness and love to flow into you with each breath. Let unconditional love flow into you with each breath. Let unconditional love flow through your being, healing all wounds and pain.

Then focus on your loved ones and send them love, peace and kindness. Then send out love to everyone who needs love and healing. Relax and breath deeply as the energy flows through you.

Get up and go about your day after feeling reenergized, refreshed, and reconnected to your inner world and higher self.

Some of the thoughts to keep in mind:

🖐 What animals have I seen lately that stick out in my mind?

🖐 Have I seen them more than once, was there something unusual about their presence around me?

🖐 Have I seen the same numbers randomly over any time period that seem significant?

🖐 Have I had any dreams where a particular symbol or sign stands out?

Start a notebook or journal where you jot down your experiences or thoughts daily, you will be surprised at the patterns that appear.

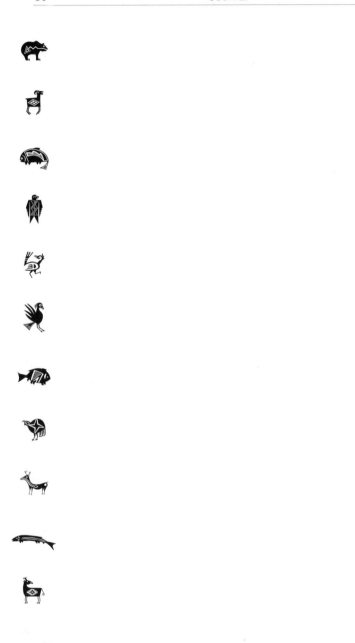

Signs and Symbol Dictionary

Ace
- This could be symbolic of a person excelling at something or a sign of hidden talents or a new beginning at some level.

Acorn
- A good sign for self potential, prosperity fruitfulness, life, fertility and immortality.

Airplane
- Can be sign of soaring to new heights, freedom, expansion, high ideals or spiritual ideals.

Altar
- Usually an altar is a symbol for the time and place where a person becomes holy or performs something holy.

Albatross
- This bird of the sea may symbolize creativity, inspiration, mothering, nurturing energies, and tells us to be alert for omens and signs.

Amethyst
- Symbolizes temperance, peace, humility, and piety. The Greeks believed that it promoted sobriety. These stones were thought to promote good and clear dreams.

Amber
- A stone that often was thought to be protective. In

Greece this stone was believed to bring you closer to the divine and your spiritual nature.

Anchor
- May symbolize strength and security, hope, consistency and fidelity.

Angel
- A sign or message from God; a special symbol of pure love.

Ankh
- Egyptian symbol of spiritual wisdom, healing and love.

Ant
- Is usually a sign to be more patient and industrious.

Ape
- In Far East a symbol of wisdom, sacred sign to some West African tribes. In many cultures it represents mischief and curiosity. In modern day communication and expression are common interpretations.

Apple
- A sign of healing potential, health, vitality and wholesomeness. In the Celtic folklore, an apple is the fruit of knowledge, magic and prophecy.

Ark
- The symbol of safety and protection, salvation and symbol of regeneration.

Arrow
- This usually is a sign of a clear direction or a straight course ahead in life.

Ax
- Has many meanings throughout time. It is a sign of wielding power with certainty, or cutting away that which is not needed—to make room for new growth.

Baggage
- Can be a sign of things, thoughts, or attitudes that you carry around that aren't necessary.

Baby
- A sign of new beginnings, new spiritual awareness, new with yourself, growth and creativity.

Badger
- May symbolize aggressive behavior, willingness to fight for what you want.

Ball
- Could signify a sign of completion, wholeness or unity.

Balloon
- Symbolizes joy, soaring to new personal heights.

Basket
- Symbolizes mastery, sometimes the womb, fertility, wholeness, togetherness with heavenly rule.

Basement
- Can symbolize the base or root of a problem with which you are struggling. Sometimes it represents a person's subconscious mind.

Bat
- This is a significant sign in many cultures. In Africa it can have a dual symbolic significance-clear-sightedness ; or someone is an enemy of the light. In China the bat is symbolic of long life and happiness. In the native traditions of the Americas the bat symbolizes shamanistic initiation and rebirth. Trust your intuition when you see a bat.

Beach
- Usually means balance in life; Often beaches can mean purifying and rejuvenating.

Bear
- Symbolic of the power of Mother Earth, introspection and renewal. Can represent protective mothering, female aspect of force and power. Many Native Americans consider the bear the totem of the healer. In the Celtic world the bear was the symbol of the warrior, and had spiritual authority. In India, the cave symbolizes the cave of

Brahma. Brahma's cave symbolizes the pineal gland that sits in the center of the four lobes of the brain.

Beaver
- Symbolizes building your dreams, taking action. Possibly a sign of prosperity through your own efforts.

Bed
- Can be symbolic of new life, rejuvenation, relaxation, nurturing, security, safety, comfort, a place of rest or healing.

Bee
- In many ancient cultures the bee symbolized royalty. In Greece the bee represented the soul. Bees became the symbol of resurrection for many cultures around the world. To the Oracle at Delphi, bees symbolized souls because they swarmed together—they thought that souls traveled together. Bees can symbolize diligence and industry. In Greece bees stood for work and productivity.

Beetles
- They can symbolize good luck or like the scarab in Egypt, eternal life and renewal.

Bell
- Symbolizes the divine voice that proclaims the truth, especially the Buddhist, Hindu, Islamic and Christian traditions. Can be a sign of personal attunement. Can be a warning to be alert. Can also be a sign of joy coming into your life.

Bird's eggs
- Symbolizes new beginnings, joy.

Black
- Symbolic of the unknown, your shadow, or the mysteries of your subconscious. The Chinese see black as a symbol of good. In many ancient traditions black was connected to earth and maternal symbolism. In modern times many used black for mourning or depression.

Bluebird
- Symbolic of transformation, bird of transition, happiness and fertility.

Blue Jay
- Often symbolic of being assertive, reflecting proper and improper uses of power. They are also considered signs of protection.

Blue
- Symbolic of spiritual healing, soothing, mystical perceptions in life, the subconscious, the feminine, deep secrets, conscious mind.

Boar
- In ancient times it sometimes meant spiritual authority. It has many meanings so listen to your intuition to see which one of these fits your encounter or dream. Throughout time boars have symbolized fidelity, strength, fertility, and family protection. The Celtic traditions connected the boar to prophecy, protection and magical powers. It can also symbolize action in whatever situation you find yourself in.

Boat
- A boat can represent your emotional body or emotional journey through life. Water can represent your emotions, and the boat shows you how you are maneuvering through your feelings. Sometimes symbolizes a journey ahead.

Books
- Can be a sign of wisdom, knowledge and the lessons in life.

Box
- May symbolize self imposed limitations.

Bread
- Usually symbolizes life; physical and spiritual nourishment.

Bridge
- This can be a powerful symbol for change and transition. You might be going from one experience to another. A passage of some type is about to occur, safely.

Bubble
- Can symbolize childlike joy and exuberance, or play. May be a message to lighten up and enjoy your life.

Buffalo
- Symbolic of abundance, great powers, harvest, plenty, pray, gratitude. Telling you to be humble enough to ask for what you need and grateful for what you receive.

Bull
- Symbolizes great strength, force, and power. Step into your power. You have the power you need. Financial abundance.

Butterfly
- Symbolizes new beginnings. Rebirth and transformation, joy and bliss. In many ancient cultures the butterfly represented the soul.

Cake
- Celebration, sweetness of life and accomplishment are the main significance of this symbol.

Cactus
- May be symbolic for a prickly situation. Another meaning a cactus represents someone or something that can't be touched. Is there someone in your life you are afraid to touch or someone who is afraid to be touched by you?

Camel
- Usually a symbol for endurance and perseverance, especially during hard times in your life. It can also symbolize finding a way through a very difficult situation and being successful.

Canal
- Symbolic of change, birth process, movement in a controlled way.

Candle
- A symbol of light; connection to the Great Spirit. Spiritual Life force or inner light.

Canyon
- A symbol of a seemingly impossible chasm or it can represent a vast opening of the unconscious.

Captain
- Symbolic of taking control of your life, situation or destiny.

Cards
- Symbolic of learning how to play the game of life or if they are tarot cards, the cards hold your future.

Caribou
- May represent action, success through movement. Travel.

Carpenter
- Symbolic of building or rebuilding some aspect of your life either figuratively or literally.

Castle
- Symbolic of home, the magical realm, a fortress (a place of safety) refuge, protection.

Cat
- Symbolic of the feminine essence, deep intuitive self, independence, grace and power.

Caterpillar
- Symbolizes good luck and new birth. A gift may be offered. . . creative inspiration—get ready for new project, or new growth requires shedding of the old.

Cave
- Powerful symbol with a range of meanings. Symbolic for the unconscious, spiritual wealth, security of the womb, safety from life's hardships, feminine symbol, heart of the world, entrance to the underworld, and esoteric wisdom.

Cemetery
- Usually represents rest, peace and completion of some form (not usually death).

Chain
- Symbolic of the strength that many links connected equally can create.

Chalice
- Abundance, joy, connected to the heart. Sacred and holy symbolism, and the chalice might represent the journey of the Holy Grail and Christ.

Chameleon
- Signifies adaptability, flexibility and changeable.

Chipmunk
- Symbolic of work, play, storing up for winter, and understanding the treasures of the earth.

Church
- Symbolic of faith, love, hope, safety and a sanctuary . . .

Circus
- Signifies laughter, joy and games.

Cliff
- Usually a sign of a big change in one's life. Maybe taking a risk where there aren't any guarantees or certainties. Take that leap of faith, make the decision that feels right.

Clouds
- Powerful symbols for the sacred mysteries in many cultures. Messages from Spirit or the Divine, often symbols of happiness or peace.

Cobra
- In India these snakes were guardian symbols, usually benevolent. Cobras often appear as guardians of shrines, sources of water or of treasures.

Cobwebs
- Might be a sign of hidden talents or memories. Ask yourself what talents are unused?

Cocoon
- A symbol of potential awaiting transformation. Growing

in a protected, closed state before a great change and growth.

Collision
- May mean that you are dealing with many conflicts in your life. Slowdown, take time to evaluate your life.

Condor
- May signal a time of rebirth and lifting up of the spirit. They are symbols of rising above the limitations of life, of spiritual growth and communion with God or Spirit. If a condor appears you are entering a time of great protection and are learning about the ancient mysteries of life and death.

Coyote
- Often called the trickster. Coyote is a sacred symbol. Usually he is telling you to develop your sense of humor, and to learn to laugh at yourself—don't take yourself too seriously.

Comet
- Symbolic for tremendous personal and spiritual expansion.

Cow
- Symbol for peace, patience and endurance. Regenerating forces of the Universe. Maternal nourishment.

Crab
- Symbol for hidden and protected sensitivity. In ancient China the crab was sacred and thought to bring good luck and repel evil.

Crane
- Heralds the change of old ways, or patterns. Longevity, honor, justice, spiritual power, prosperity, ability to communicate clearly, beauty and stamina.

Crash
- Symbol telling you to slow down, assess your present situation.

Cricket
- Symbol for long life, happiness, sensitive intuition, blessings in the home and relationships.

Crocodile
- The Egyptians had several interpretations—one was fury and viciousness. The other significance was power and wisdom. Look beneath the surface and see what the truth of the situation is.

Cross
- Has taken many forms and meanings throughout history. The cross was a mystical symbol before the time of Christ. In ancient traditions it represented a holy balance of opposites, the earthly and celestial.

Crystal
- Powerful symbol of clarity and spiritual energy. It is the sign of the mystic. Listen carefully to this symbol.

Cup
- Usually a symbol of overflowing abundance (either materially or emotionally).

Dawn
- May symbolize a new beginning , awakening, illumination and seeing the light. It is time to make a fresh start.

Death
- Usually it symbolizes transformation, the death of old patterns. Clearing the way for rebirth, and makes way for new growth in your life. this sign may also relates to fear of death, either your own or someone else.

Deer
- Can symbolize gentleness, love and compassion. Use the power of gentleness to touch the hearts and minds of the wounded beings in your life. The lesson of the deer is to love people as they are today.

Desert
- Symbolic for spiritual rejuvenation, purification and

emotional clarity. For some it is a symbol or sign of loneliness, isolation and desolation. Trust your felling and see what this symbol means for you.

Dog
- Usually a sign of friendship, protection, guidance and loyalty.

Dolphin
- Usually are signs of joy, playfulness, spontaneity and spiritual enlightenment. Powerful communication, mental telepathy.

Door
- This is considered a significant symbol. It may mean a great opportunity for self discovery or a new adventure. A new phase of life. an open door means you are ready for a new beginning. A closed door means that it is not the right time for something yet.

Dove
- This is a sign of peace, love, harmony and inspired thought.

Dragonfly
- Transformation and change. Dragonflies symbolize the winds of change, communication, wisdom, and enlightenment. Dragonfly helps you understand your dreams, break down illusions and see the truth in situations.

Dragon
- A complex and universal symbol often stands for life force and great potency. It signals a time when you should step into your power. Often considered a guardian symbol. Opposing forces.

Drum
- Often symbolized the first sound, divine truth and speech. It is associated with lightning and thunder. To the Native American it represented the heart of the universe.

Eagle
- A very powerful symbol throughout history. Native people around the world consider the eagle the symbol of the

Great Spirit. In ancient Egypt the eagle was the symbol of the full sun and the day. It was the sign of illumination. In many ancient cultures the eagle was a messenger from the heavens. If a eagle comes to you it can signal a time of power, strength or freedom.

Earthquake
• Usually a sign that great changes are coming.

Egg
• Significant symbol of new life and new potential. Many ancient cultures had myths about the egg being the origin of the Universe. Symbol of hope and immortality.

Elephant
• Universally a symbol of power. Patience and the ability to remove obstacles. Fidelity and longevity. Wisdom.

Elf
• Mischievous. Have fun or lighten up. Stop taking life so seriously.

Emerald
• Many cultures used the emerald for its healing properties. The Egyptians considered it the jewel of love. Magic. Thought to enhance memory, sharpen wits and help predict the future.

Falcons
• Sacred gift. Slow and steady progress, keen observation.

Feather
• In ancient Egypt feathers were symbolic of winds and the gods Hathor, Osiris, Path and Amon. In Christianity feathers often meant faith and contemplation. For the Native Americans feathers were considered connections between the Great sprit and man.

Fire
• Symbolic of intuition, spiritual communication, energy and often purification. It is also a sign of our life force, power and psychic energy.

Fish
- To the ancient Babylonians, Phoenicians, Assyrians and Chinese fish were a fertility symbol and symbol of spirituality. It is a symbol of Christianity. It can also symbolize wealth, riches and food.

Flamingo
- Symbolic of cleansing, healing and filtering through the lessons of the heart ; flirtatiousness, community, soul moving from darkness to the light.

Flood
- May symbolize powerful or overwhelming emotions. Often symbolized growth and regeneration.

Flowers
- Usually symbolic of happiness, beauty, youth, vitality, and positive unfolding of a situation. Different flowers symbolize different things. The lotus, for example, stands for the soul rising from the confusion of matter into the clarity of enlightenment.

Fog
- Often stands for mystery, things hidden, mystical, confusion and secrets.

Forest
- Often stands for the female principle and the Great Mother. Abundance, growth, strength, protection, or place of refuge are common themes around the meaning of forest.

Fruit
- Often symbolized abundance, fertility, immorality, and longevity.

Fox
- Symbolic of protection, adaptability, ability to observe silently instead of action, and cunning.

Frog
- In ancient Egypt frogs were symbolic of fertility. In some cultures they were believed to bring rain; or they

were a sign of purification and cleansing. In Mayan and Aztec cultures they believed frogs could promote healing.

Garden

- May be symbolic of peace, creative activity, beauty and growth.

Glider

- Usually stands for change and going with the flow in life.

Glove

- Symbolic of protection at many levels.

Gold

- Symbolic of the sun, spirit and life. Connected to the golden light of inner peace, spirituality and goodness.

Goldfish

- The Chinese have had goldfish for thousands of years. Ponds with goldfish help to balance the home's energy, inviting peace and prosperity. When a goldfish appears peace and prosperity is promoted.

Goose

- Symbolic of the Great Mother like the swan and the duck.

Gorilla

- Powerful symbol of strength (inner strength and nobility); endeavors are solid and steady ; generosity is important.

Grain/Grains

- Seed growth, life , abundance, the staff of life and sustenance are basic meanings of this sign.

Great Blue Heron

- Reminds us to follow our own path in life. Symbolic for uniqueness; accurate advice and counsel.

Green

- Symbolic of fertility, abundance of nature, new growth, healing, prosperity and the heart.

Hawk

- Symbolic messenger, represented the soul in many cultures, victory, and a sign that tells us to pay attention to communication.

Heart
- Symbolic of love, bliss, compassion, understanding and emotions.

Hippopotamus
- A powerful symbol telling you it is time to use your creativity and heal your life. Symbolic of awakening our higher sensibilities and conscious spirit contact. The hippopotamus may signify spiritual or sacred baptism. Great power can be called on to overcome obstacles, and protect your family.

Home
- Symbolic of one's physical/or spiritual self.

Horse
- Symbolizes power, freedom, grace movement and beauty. American shaman tradition said that the spirit of the horse helped them to travel to the inner realms.

Hummingbird
- Symbolic of joy, happiness, energy, and freedom.

Jaguar
- When this cat shows up , your patience is about to be rewarded, but you need to be alert and aware when the opportunity you are waiting for occurs. The jaguar is symbolic of mastery over dimensions; great mysticism and telling you to be on the lookout for good opportunities from various directions.

Jackal
- In Egypt, Anubis was the jackal god. He was the guardian of the underworld. If the jackal appears as a sign your senses can be trusted as you maneuver through the dark inner realms or hard places in life; protection is also indicated.

Jewel
- A sign of that which is precious, brilliant and abundance. Could be a sign of coming riches or true happiness.

Kangaroo
  • Symbolic of mobility and potential of great leaps forward.

Key
  • Symbolic of new opportunities or doors opening for you; solutions might be at hand.

King
  • Can signify the archetypal man; or power and majesty, royalty; authority, self responsibility and taking charge of your own life.

Kite
  • Sign of spiritual soaring yet grounded and anchored. Freedom and joy.

Knife
  • Could symbolize cutting away either old patterns of thinking and being; or that which isn't necessary any more. The knife can be interpreted as either a creative force or of destruction depending on the situation around the symbol.

Knot
  • This sign can mean that it is time to make a commitment to the one you love.

Ladder
  • Can symbolize attaining a higher awareness or reaching new heights.

Ladybug
  • Sign of good luck. The appearance of a ladybug heralds protection, happiness, wishes being fulfilled, worries will begin to dissipate in the Universe's time. Relax and try not to push too hard.

Lake
  • The ancient Egyptians thought a lake symbolized the occult and mysterious realms. In the Celtic world the Land of the Dead was at the bottom of a lake. Water might stand for your subconscious, or the unknown.

Larks

• These birds sing while in flight. For those to whom the lark appears, the mysteries and science of sound, music and voice will become increasingly important. Throughout the Shetland Islands the lark is considered a sacred bird. When the lark appears our own song is being awakened in our life.

Letter

• Individual letters of the alphabet had mystic, symbolic importance in many ancient cultures. A letter could be a sign that information or news is coming, so pay attention.

Lily

• Symbolic of rebirth, transformation, faith and trust.

Lighthouse

• Symbolic of guidance through life's journey. Safe harbor or guiding light.

Lightning

• This powerful symbol could represent great power, a breakthrough ahead in a situation or problem. It has been a symbol in all cultures of speed, strength, awakening of your inner life force or connection to Spirit.

Lizard

• This is usually a sign for you to pay attention to your dreams. They will contain important messages for you. The lizard can also symbolize your subconscious mind, sit and listen to your inner self for information.

Lotus

• This flower may symbolize spiritual awakening. The lotus rises out of the mud, you might be coming up and out of the darkness and into the light.

Magician

• Symbolizes channeling power from the inner to the outer realms. Can symbolize the sage or the wise old man.

Mandala
- Usually symbolizes the whole self and the entire Universe. Powerful sign of harmony, beauty, and balance.

Mermaid
- May be symbolic of a magical and spiritual communion with the sea, with your emotions, and with the depths of your being or subconscious mind.

Mirror
- In China mirrors are used to reflect or dispel unfavorable influences. In folklore in different cultures the mirror is magical. Explore the magic in your life.

Moose
- Powerful symbol representing wisdom, self-esteem, joyfulness, balance, encouragement.

Moon
- Symbolic of the feminine, creativity, wholeness, deep reflection and listening to your inner self and dreams.

Mountain
- Symbolic of an attainable goal or opportunity.

Mouse
- Can be symbolic of paying attention to or dealing with details in your life. They sometimes are a sign of fear or being too timid.

Numbers
- If you see numbers over and over again you might get really quiet and ask your spirit guides what they mean for you. Here are some of the meanings:

One
- Creativity, active, self-development, independence, dynamic, pioneering, unique, unusual, ego, self, individuality.

Two
- Balance, yin and yang, dynamic attraction, partnerships, cooperation, instinctive, intuitive, passive, reactive, aware of both sides.

Three

   • Trinity, divinity, communication, expansion, growth, creativity, self-expression, travel, lucky events, social, positive thinking, generosity, multi-talented, scattered.

Four

   • Order, foundation, form, organization, home, land, security, work, deliberateness, tenacity.

Five

   • Communication, freedom, change, activity, energy, quickness, speed, experience, adventuresome, resourceful, free soul, excitement.

Six

   • Love, family, responsibility, community, balance, counseling, love of beauty, activity with home and family, service, health, self harmony, compassion, beauty, the arts, generosity, children.

Seven

   • The mind, rest, analysis, meditation, reserved, reclusive, perfectionist, personal health, birth, rebirth, spiritual strength, path of solitude, analysis, contemplation, inner life, inner wisdom.

Eight

   • Responsibility, discipline, business, infinity, material prosperity, cosmic consciousness, reward, authority, leadership, power, endurance.

Nine

   • Universal wisdom, understanding, caring, completion, inclusive, broad-minded, finishing cycles, regeneration, generosity, humanitarian, selflessness, universal compassion, tolerance and wisdom.

Ten

   • Perfection, accomplishment, solution or new beginning.

Eleven

   • Developing intuition, clarification, spiritual healing.

Twenty Two
- Unlimited potential of mastery in any area, not only spiritual but physical, emotional and mental.

Thirty- Three
- All things are possible.

Nurse
- This is usually a sign of healing , caring and nurturing.

Oak
- Symbolic of strength, solidarity, steady progress. Many traditions including Greek, Scandinavian, Russian and German cultures give significant meaning to the mighty oak tree.

Ocean
- Can be a sign to trust your intuition; or delve deeply into ancient wisdom within yourself; your subconscious mind.

Octopus
- Can be a powerful symbol of transformation. The art of Crete depicted the octopus as the mystic center of the Universe and the unfolding of creation.

Orange
- Powerful color that symbolizes optimism, expansiveness, emotional balance, enthusiasm, change, confidence, self-motivation, happiness, warmheartedness and tolerance.

Otter
- Usually signifies balanced female energy, power, joyfulness, ability to share easily, trustworthiness, and learn to flow with the waters of the Universe.

Oyster
- Can be symbolic of hidden beauty; small irritations in life can be transformed into something of beauty; great value hidden from sight.

Panda
- Can be symbolic of tranquility, lovable and everything that the Bear stands for.

Parrot
- Can be symbolic of the jungle, color and verbal expression. Find your own individuality and express it.

Peacock
- In ancient Rome this bird was the soul-bird of the empress and her princesses. The Persian court was the "Peacock Throne", and peacocks are also associated with the thrones of the Hindu god Indra, and the Buddhist Amitaka.

Pearl
- Symbolizes light and femininity, the moon, fertility, spiritual wisdom. The Romans wore pearls to honor Isis and used them as protection against evil, the goddess Aphrodite wore pearls.

Pink
- Usually symbolic of love, purity, innocence, joy of life, vitality and tenderness.

Piano
- Can be symbolic of creative expression through sound and raising your energy through musical octaves.

Pond
- Symbolic of emotions and intuition, usually calm, clear emotions if the pond is calm and clear. Peaceful.

Porcupine
- Reminds us to have faith, trust, and humility. Symbolic of the need to have faith and honor the wonder of life and appreciation of each new day as an adventure.

Prairie Dog
- May signify a time in your life when you need to quiet your mind and body. Basic needs of a regular life style, nourishing food, enough sleep are all connected to the message of the Prairie Dog.

Purple or Violet
- Usually symbolizes beauty, serenity, spirituality, power, sensitivity.

Quartz
  • Stands for celestial element in some cultures' rites, and gives power and clarity to your hopes, wishes, and dreams.

Rabbit
  • Can be symbolic of prosperity, fertility, abundance, learn to face your fears head on, Stop, breathe, relax and learn to focus and tackle one project at a time.

Raccoon
  • Is considered the protector of the underdog and helpful for the sick, elderly or young.

Radio
  • Symbolic of dimensions and experiences available to a person. Pay attention to your inner dials; communication and guidance from other sources.

Rainbow
  • Symbolic of blessings, your relationships, ventures being blessed by Spirit. Can be a powerful sign of celebration, joy, hope and end of difficulties.

Ring
  • Can be a powerful sign of the continuous circle of life. Can be a sign of wholeness, unity, completion, friendship, engagement, marriage, commitment and eternal love.

Red
  • Powerful symbol of creation, passion, strength, anger, sexuality, sensuality, aggression, anger, life and power.

River
  • Can symbolize movement, rhythm of change, or flow of life.

Rose
  • A universal sign of love and beauty. The rose can symbolize the mystic center of the heart, the emblem of the goddess Venus and the divine beings.

Seeds
  • Usually symbolic for new beginnings either physically, spiritually, mentally or emotionally.

Salmon

- May symbolize inner wisdom, determination, ability to overcome all obstacles and stay on true course no matter how difficult it appears to be.

Shoes

- Can be symbolic of taking positive steps forward in your life. Being grounded.

Snake

- Can be a significant sign of healing, transformation, resurrection, rebirth, spiritual awakening and spiritual healing.

Star

- Symbolic of light, guidance, insight, following the light within, hope.

Squirrel

- Might be symbolic of being patient and prepared for your life.

Stork

- Symbolic of happiness, contentment, birth of a new project or baby, new idea that will grow in your life.

Sun

- Symbolic of power, strength, clarity, inner light. In many cultures throughout the world the sun is the symbol for God, Christ or the Great Spirit.

Temple

- Usually symbolic of a sanctuary either in the physical or within yourself.

Tiger

- A powerful symbol of energy, strength and power. This animal was revered in many countries, especially China.

Train

- Can signify the power to accomplish your goals. Opportunities are being presented in your life. Avoiding trains could be a sign of avoiding opportunities that are being presented.

Tide
- Symbolic of the ebb and flow of life (often connected to the flow of your emotions). Allowing change to safely be in your life without fear.

Treasure
- A sign of inner gifts and wealth from spirit.

Trees
- Significant symbol throughout the world. Can be a symbol of your life and growth. A tree can pertain to your family. A fruit tree is a very good symbol for positive efforts in your life.

Umbrella
- Symbol of protection from danger.

Unicorn
- Symbolic of creativity, spiritual unfoldment, Jesus, magic, joy, childlike innocence and purity.

Water
- Powerful symbol throughout the world. It is usually connected to emotions, feelings, intuition, the subconscious mind, the feminine, new life, rebirth, fertility, and new creative potential.

Whale
- Symbolic of the ability to tap into the Universal Mind of the Great Spirit, to help people remember ancient knowledge and wisdom. Uniqueness. Powerful communication and wisdom. Developing balance of emotional and physical bodies.

White
- Symbolizes protection, spiritual advancement, openness to Spirit and purity.

Wheel
- Symbolic of ever turning, ever-changing nature of life. Everything changes.

Contributors

The following people contributed generously to this book and are willing to be contacted:

Angeles Arrien
Cross-cultural anthropologist, author, educator, consultant, seminar leader and speaker.
P.O. Box 2077
Sausalito, CA 94966
415-33-5050
www.angelesarrien.com
e-mail: aarrien@aol.com

Julie Claire Bahne
Lumina/Life Art & Essence
P.O. Box 254, Hanalei, Hawaii, 96714
808-826-2528

Dorothe Blackmere
Author, teacher and internationally known psychic
4935 Durham
Boulder, CO 80301
303-530-3526

Gloria Brown
Artist and book illustrator
Pagosa Springs, CO
May be contacted through Synchronicity Publishing

Arielle Ford
Author, and Publicist
1250 Prospect St. #0-5, LaJolla, CA 92034
www.fordsisters.com
e-mail: fordgroup@aol.com
The Ford Group is a book publicity firm specializing in
spiritual, self-help, and mind-body medicine books.

Paola Harris
Journalist, teacher and photographer
www.utenti.tripod.it/paolaharris
e-mail: paolaharris@hotmail.com

Suzanne M. Humes
NAPRA (Networking Alternatives for Publishers, Retailers
and Artists)
P.O. Box 9, 109 North Beach Rd., Eastbound. WA. 98245
360-376-2702
e-mail: napraexec@rockisland.com

Deb Jordan
Owner of Phoenix Phyre Books
World Imports, Books & Services
Independent Metaphysical bookstore, psychic services,
bi-monthly newspaper, Phyre Talk, lectures & workshops.
282 N. El Camino Real, Ste. G & H
Encintas, CA 92024
760-436-7740
www.phoenixphyre.com

Frank Joseph
Author, lecturer and teacher
May be contacted in care of Ancient American Magazine
P.O. Box 370, Colfax, WI 54730
e-mail: joseph@ancientamerican.com

Nancy Lee
Talk Show Host
2519 S. shields, 1-k
PMB #112, Fort collins, CO 80526
970-472-9104
e-mail: lightson@nancylee.net
Visionary Communication of the Rockies, Show—"Lights On with Nancy Lee" Nancy is an internationally known spiritual clairvoyant.

Danielle Lin
Talk Show Host
P.O. Box 9364Salt Lake City, Utah 84109
801-278-9669
www.daniellelin.com

Denise Linn
Author, Teacher and Lecturer
P.O. Box 759
Paso Robles, CA 93447

Kate Solisti-Mattelon & Patrice Mattelon
Authors, animal communicators and teachers.
505-466-6958
e-mail: solmat@earthlink.net

Susan Miller
Internationally known astrologer
Please contact her at www.astrologyzone.com.

Raleigh Pinskey
The Raleigh Group—A Viz-Ability Marketing and PR Company.
www.promoteyourself.com
Helping you to get more than just your 15 minutes of fame

and helping your to get your message in front of your buying audience.
800-249-7322
e-mail: raleigh@promoteyourself.com

Candace Powers
Numerologist
www.numerologybycandice.com
303-546-2727

Marilyn Ross
Author, Speaker, co-founder of SPAN
P.O. Box 1306
Buena Vista, CO 81211
www.SPANnet.org

Ed Rubenstein
Author, and psychologist
231 Sage Way
Marshal, N.C. 28753
868-649-3870

Gayle Seminara-Mandel
Owner of Transitions Bookplace
1000 W North
Chicago, IL 60620
312-951-7523
6000 sq. ft bookstore with 4000 sq. ft. learning center dedicated to personal growth, inward exploration and the pursuit of spirituality.

Jacquelyn Small
Author, lecturer and teacher
3930 Bee Caves Rd., Austin, Texas 78746
512-327-2214. 512-327-2795
e-mail: jacquiesm@aol.com

Sandra Wales
Author, teacher and lecturer
May be contacted through The Writer's Block, Inc.
1329 Stevenson Rd.
Franklin, KY 42134
270-598-5861

Dottie Walters
Author, International Speaker, Runs Walters Speaker Services,
publishes *Sharing Ideas Magazine* for speakers.
P.O. Box 398, Glendora, California, 91740
626 -335-8069
e-mail: dottie@walters-intl.com

Bibliography

Adrienne, Carol. *The Purpose of Your Life*. New York: Eagle Brook, 1998.

Andrews, Ted. Animal-Wise: *The Spirit Language and Signs of Nature*. Jackson, Tennessee: Dragonhawk Publishing, 1999.

Arguelles, Jose. *The Mandala*. Boston: Shambala Press, 1985.Arrien, Angeles. *Signs of Life*. Jeremy P. Tarcher/Putnam, New York,1998.

Barker, Graeme & Tom Rasmussen. *The Etruscans*. Maleden, Massachusetts: Blackwell Publishers, 1998.

Bayley, Harold. *The Lost Language of Symbolism,* Vols. 1 & 2, New York; Carol Publishing Group, 1989.

Becker, Udo. *The Continuum Encyclopedia of Symbols*. New York: Continuum Publishing, 2000.

Blum, Ralph. *The Book of Runes*. New York; St. Martin's Press, 1982.

Bolen, Jean Shimoda. *The Tao of Psychology: Synchronicity and The Self.* New York: Harper & Row. 1979.

Bruce-Mitford, Miranda. *The Illustrated Book of Signs & Symbols*. New York: DK Publishing, Inc., 1996.

Carson, David, and Jamie Sams. *Medicine Cards: The Discovery of Power Through the Ways of Animals.* Santa Fe, NM: Bear & Company, 1988.

Chevalier, Jean & Alain Gheerbrant, *The Penguin Dictionary of Symbols*. London: Penguin Books, 1996. Translated by John Buchanan-Brown.

Combs, Allan & Mark Holland. *Synchronicity: Science, Myth & The Trickster.* New York: Paragon House, 1990. Cousineau, Phil. Soul Moments. Berkeley, California: Conrai Press, 1997.

Curry, Helen. *The Way of the Labyrinth.* New York: Penguin Compass, 2000.

Fontana, David. *The Secret Language of Symbols.* San Francisco: Chronicle books, 1993.

Hopcke, Robert H. *There Are No Accidents. Synchronicity and the Stories of Our Lives.* New York: Riverhead Books, 1997.

Ifrah, Georges. *The Universal History of Numbers.* New York: John Wiley & Sons Inc., 2000.

Javane, Faith. *Master Numbers—Cycles of Divine Order.* Atglen, Pennsylvania: Whitford Press, 1988.

Joseph, Frank. *Synchronicity & You—Understanding the Role of Meaningful Coincidence in Your Life.* Boston: Element Books, Inc., 1999.

Jung, Carl G. *Synchronicity: An Acausal Connecting Principal.* New York: Princeton University Press, 1973.

_____. *Man and His Symbols.* Garden city, New Jersey: Doubleday, 1964.

Koestler, Arthur. *The Roots of Coincidence.* New York: Random House, 1973.

Lawlor, Robert. *Sacred Geometry.* New York: The Crossroad Publishing Company, 1982.

Linn, Denise. *The Secret Language of Signs.* New York: Ballantine Books, 1996.

Mansfield, Victor. *Synchronicity, Science & Soul-Making.* Peru, Illinois: Open Court Publishing, 1995.

Peat, F. David. *Synchronicity: The Bridge Between Matter and Mind.* New York: Bantam, 1987.

Progoff, Ira. *Jung, Synchronicity, and Human Destiny.* New York: Dell, 1973.

_____. *The Symbolic and The Real.* New York: Julian Press, Inc.

Redfield, James. *The Celestine Prophecy: An Adventure.* New York: Warner Books, 1993.

Sands, Helen Raphael. *The Healing Labyrinth.* New York: Barron's, 2001.

Sheldrake, Rupert. *Morphic Resonance & The Presence of the Past, The Habits of Nature.* Rochester, Vermont: Park Street Press, 1988.

Talbot, Michael. *The Holographic Universe.* New York: Harper-Collins, 1991.

Telihard de Chardin, Pierre. *The Phenomenon of Man.* New York: Harper & Row, 1959.

Thurston, Mark. *Synchronicity as Spiritual Guidance.* Virginia Beach, Virginia: A.R.E. Press, 1997.

Tresidder, Jack. *Symbols and Their Meanings.* London: Duncan Baird Publishers, 2000.

Vaughn, Alan. *Incredible Coincidences: The Baffling World of Synchronicity.* New York: Ballantine, 1979.

Walter, Katya. *Tao of Chaos—DNA & The I Ching: Unlocking the Code of the Universe.* Boston: Element Books, 1994.

Weiss, Brian . *Many Lives, Many Masters.* New York: Warner Books, 1990.

_____. *Messages From The Masters.* New York: Warner Books, Inc., 2000.

_____. *Only Love Is Real.* New York: Warner Books, Inc., 1996.

Yogananda, Paramahansa. *Autobiography of A Yogi.* Los Angeles: Self-Realization Fellowship, 1993.

Patricia Rose Upczak has worn many hats professionally over the last twenty years. She designed and developed the special education program for learning disabled students at a large high school in Boulder, Colorado in 1975. In 1985 she simultaneously became involved in writing and Reiki. She teaches Reiki and other seminars around the country. Her other books, STEVE and REIKI A WAY OF LIFE are available in bookstores, on Amazon.com , through Synchronicity Publishing or by calling 1-800-929-7889.

For information about Patricia's workshops and seminars please write or email your request to:

Patricia Rose Upczak
P.O. Box 927
Nederland, CO 80466
e-mail address: synchron@csd.net

Books from
Synchronicity Publishing

To order copies of Synchronicity, Signs & Symbols ($13.99—ISBN# 18919554-19-0), please fill out the form in the back of the book and return with your payment and $3.75 for shipping and handling.

You may also order REIKI A WAY OF LIFE—A powerful guide for all people interested in alternative healing methods. ($13.99—ISBN# 1891554-18-1) or STEVE, a grieving process book for families ($12.99—ISBN# 1-891554-15-8). Many people grow and transform dramatically through their grieving over the death of a loved one. This book is about a remarkable family and their healing.

Order Form

I wish to order:

_____ copies of _____ at $_____ each.

_____ copies of _____ at $_____ each.

_____ copies of _____ at $_____ each.

Book Total $ _____

For shipping and handleing, please add $3.75
Colorado residents please add
appropriate sale tax on total. $ _____

Total $ _____

Payment:

    ○ Check   ○ Money Order

    ○ Visa   ○ Mastercard

Account Number _____

Expiration Date _____

Please print exact name appearing on credit card:

_____

Signature _____

You may also fax your order if you are paying by credit card:
303-258-7917.

Thank you. We appreciate your business.